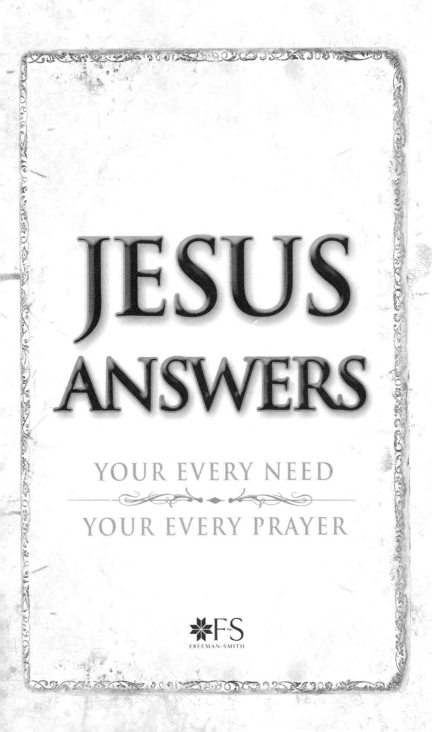

# JESUS
# ANSWERS

## YOUR EVERY NEED

## YOUR EVERY PRAYER

✳FS

FREEMAN-SMITH

Copyright © 2013 by Freeman–Smith, a division of Worthy Media, Inc.

www.JesusAnswers.me

ISBN 978-1-60587-527-9

Published by Freeman-Smith, a division of Worthy Media, Inc.,
134 Franklin Road, Suite 200, Brentwood, Tennessee 37027.

Library of Congress Control Number: 2013913923

Scripture references marked KJV are from the Holy Bible, King James Version

Scripture references marked NKJV are from the Holy Bible, New King James Version. Copyright © 1982 by Thomas Nelson, Inc. Used by permission.

Scripture references marked NCV are from the New Century Version®. Copyright © 1987, 1988, 1991 by Word Publishing, a division of Thomas Nelson, Inc. All rights reserved. Used by permission.

Scripture references marked HCSB are from the Holman Christian Standard Bible™ Copyright © 1999, 2000, 2001 by Holman Bible Publishers. Used by permission.

Scripture references marked NIV are from the Holy Bible, New International Version®. Copyright © 1973, 1978, 1984 International Bible Society. Used by permission of Zondervan. All rights reserved.

Scripture references marked NLT are from the Holy Bible. New Living Translation. Copyright © 1996 Tyndale Charitable Trust. Used by permission of Tyndale House Publishers.

Scripture references marked NASB are from the New American Standard Bible®. Copyright © 1960, 1962, 1963, 1968, 1971, 1972, 1973, 1975, 1977, 1995 by The Lockman Foundation. Used by permission.

Scripture references marked MSG are from the Message. Copyright © 1993, 1994, 1995, 1996, 2000, 2001, 2002. Used by permission of NavPress Publishing Group.

Cover Design by Kim Russell / Wahoo Designs
Page Layout by Bart Dawson

Printed in the United States of America

1 2 3 4 5—QGF—17 16 15 14 13

# TABLE OF CONTENTS

# INTRODUCTION

When we have questions, where do we turn? It's tempting to turn to the world for answers, but the earthly value system is flawed. We're sometimes tempted to turn to science, or to psychology, or to philosophy for solutions. But these fields of study, as helpful as they may be, often lack the eternal truths that can provide permanent solutions to our lives. Thankfully, we have a source of wisdom we can always depend on—a source of answers that never fails. That source is God's Word. And if we're wise, we turn to it, first and always, for the answers to life's biggest questions. But God's Word is not just a book. God's ultimate Truth is Jesus Christ, and He is alive today to hear our prayers and speak to our hearts.

Being a follower of Jesus in modern society isn't easy. Our world is filled with distractions and temptations that are probably more intense than other generations faced. And the world is changing so rapidly that, at times, it seems difficult to catch our breath and keep our balance.

Thankfully, in a rapidly changing world, God remains unchanged. In a society that is built on the shifting sands of popular culture, God's truth remains constant. In a time of uncertainty and doubt, God's promises are sure and true and can be trusted.

This text is intended to reassure you of the eternal promises that are found in God's Word and of God's never-ending love for you. These pages will remind you that Jesus can answer every big question we humans face. And may you, in turn, share those answers with the friends and family members whom God has placed along your path.

*Jesus answered,*
*"I am the way and the truth and the life.*
*No one comes to the Father except through me."*

—

JOHN 14:6 NIV

# 1

ABILITY

# I AM NOT LIVING UP TO MY POTENTIAL

*Sure, I have abilities, I guess.*
*But what does God really want me*
*to do with them?*

## THE HEART OF JESUS ANSWERS:

*The man who had received the five talents brought the other five. "Master," he said, "you entrusted me with five talents. See, I have gained five more." His master replied, "Well done, good and faithful servant! You have been faithful with a few things; I will put you in charge of many things. Come and share your master's happiness."*

MATTHEW 25:20-21 NIV

JESUS

---

God knew exactly what He was doing when He created you and gave you a unique set of abilities and opportunities. And now, God wants you to use those talents for the glory of His kingdom. So here's the big question: will you choose to use your talents, or not?

Your Heavenly Father wants you to be a faithful steward of the gifts He has given you. But you live in a society that may encourage you to do otherwise. You face countless temptations to squander your time, your resources, and your talents. So you must be keenly aware of the inevitable distractions that can waste your time, your energy, and your opportunities.

God has blessed you with many opportunities to serve Him, and He has given you every tool you need to do so. Today, accept this challenge: value the talent that God has given you, nourish it, make it grow, and share it with the world, beginning now.

God has given you abilities and opportunities. Discover those abilities and develop them. The Lord has work for you to do . . . now!

**You are the only person on earth
who can use your ability.**

ZIG ZIGLAR

## THE HEART OF JESUS PRAYS:

*Father, help this beloved child of Yours realize that all good talents and gifts come from You, and can be used to further Your kingdom. May this one work to develop the abilities— and take advantage of the opportunities—that You've given. May Your Spirit so fill this one that when others see good things happen, they'll always give praise to You.*

2

---

# WHAT CAN I EXPECT FROM MY FAITH?

*What does it mean for a Christian like me
to receive God's abundance?*

## THE HEART OF JESUS ANSWERS:

*I have come that they may have life, and that they may have it more abundantly.*

JOHN 10:10 NKJV

JESUS

G od sent His Son so all of us might enjoy the abundant life Jesus promises in the words of John 10:10. But God's gifts are not guaranteed; those of us who follow Christ must ask for them. As you plan for your days, weeks, and months, you may wonder, "What kind of life does God intend for me?" You can find the answer in God's promise of abundance: when we accept that promise and live according to God's commandments, we're eternally blessed.

Whether or not we accept God's abundance is, of course, up to each of us. When we entrust our hearts and our days to the One who created us, we experience God's peace. But, when we turn our thoughts and our energies away from God's commandments, we inevitably forfeit the earthly peace and spiritual blessings we might have otherwise.

What is your focus today? Are you focused on God's Word and His will for your life? Or are you focused on the distractions of a difficult, temptation-filled world? If you sincerely seek the spiritual abundance that your Savior offers, then you should follow Him completely and without reservation. When you do, you will receive the love, the life, and the abundance that He has promised.

---

**Instead of living a black-and-white existence, we'll be released into a Technicolor world of vibrancy and emotion when we more accurately reflect His nature to the world around us.**

BILL HYBELS

---

## THE HEART OF JESUS PRAYS:

*Father, help Your children know that You do not just want them to experience the joy of abundant life during their future in heaven...but that You also want them to know the wonder, the blessings, and awe of overwhelmingly great life here and now, on earth. May Your Spirit fill this one, for whom You have provided so graciously, and may You help this one find the specific provisions You intend to share.*

# 3

ACCEPTING CHRIST

# A WALK TO REMEMBER

*I know the Bible teaches that we need to*
*build a relationship with Jesus.*
*But what does that really mean in my life?*

## THE HEART OF JESUS ANSWERS:

*If people love me, they will obey my teaching. My Father will love them, and we will come to them and make our home with them.*

JOHN 14:23 NCV

JESUS

Your decision to let Christ reign over your heart is the pivotal decision of your life. It will effect every area of your life, and it's a decision you can't ignore. This is also a decision that only you can make.

God's love for you is deeper and more profound than you can even imagine. God's love for you is so great that He sent His only Son to this earth to die for your sins and to offer you the priceless gift of eternal life—living in the amazing world of heaven when your time on earth is over. But you must decide whether or not to accept God's gift. Will you ignore it or embrace it? Will you return it or neglect it? Will you say "Yes!" to Christ's love and build a lifelong friendship with Him, or will you turn away from Him?

Accept God's gift now: let His Son rule over your heart, your thoughts, and your life. Don't wait! Turn to Him now! Jesus loves you and has sacrificed for you. Now, He asks you to welcome Him into your heart today.

---

**Turn your life over to Christ today,
and your life will never be the same.**
BILLY GRAHAM

---

## THE HEART OF JESUS PRAYS:

*Father, I pray for this child You love. I pray that Your Spirit will break down any walls that distance this one from a relationship with You. Help this one to have the courage to choose the exciting life You have prepared. May this one seek You every day and in every circumstance of life.*

# 4

## ACTION

# I NEED TO
# GET THINGS DONE

*If I'm depending on God's grace,*
*are actions really that important?*

## THE HEART OF JESUS ANSWERS:

*Even so every good tree bringeth forth good fruit; but a corrupt tree bringeth forth evil fruit. A good tree cannot bring forth evil fruit, neither can a corrupt tree bring forth good fruit. Every tree that bringeth not forth good fruit is hewn down, and cast into the fire. Wherefore by their fruits ye shall know them.*

MATTHEW 7:17-20 KJV

JESUS

---

The old saying is both familiar and true: actions speak louder than words. So we should always make sure that what we do demonstrates the changes God can make in the lives of people who walk with Him.

The Creator calls each of us to act according to His will and with respect for His commandments. We must realize that it is never enough simply to hear God's instructions; or even to hear them and agree with them. We also need to live by them. And it's never enough to just sit around waiting while others do the Father's work here on earth—we must also get busy.

Each of us is responsible to do God's work as He guides us. And when we do, our loving Heavenly

Father rewards our efforts with an overflowing harvest in this world and in the next.

Because you will be known by your actions rather than your words, it's always the right time to do the right thing.

---

**Every time you refuse to face up to life and its problems, you weaken your character.**
E. STANLEY JONES

---

## THE HEART OF JESUS PRAYS:

*Father, it's so easy for humans to cut corners. It's easy for them to believe that other people know their hearts are in the right place, so their behavior at any given moment doesn't really matter very much. I pray that Your Spirit will fill the precious child who's reading these words. I pray that You will empower this one to do what is right and pleasing to You at all times.*

# 5

---

# I CAN'T SAY "NO"

---

*I know that addiction is a physical problem.*
*But does it affect us spiritually?*

## THE HEART OF JESUS ANSWERS:

*It is written: You shall worship the Lord your God, and Him alone you shall serve.*

JESUS

＊＊＊

O ur society glamorizes the use of alcohol, drugs, cigarettes, and other addictive substances. Why? Money. Simply put, addictive substances are big money makers, so suppliers (of both legal and illegal substances) work overtime to make sure that people like you sample their products. The suppliers need a steady stream of new customers because the old ones are dying off (fast). So it's no surprise that they engage in a no-holds-barred struggle to find new users—or more accurately, new abusers.

If you want to wreck your self-esteem—not to mention your health—let yourself become an addict. But if you want to enhance your sense of self-worth, treat addictive substances like the life-destroying poisons that they are.

Addiction is slavery, so please beware of the things that ensnare.

# Addiction is the most powerful psychic enemy of humanity's desire for God.

—

GERALD MAY

⸻

## THE HEART OF JESUS PRAYS:

*Father, addictions can sneak up on Your children so quietly and subtly. After all, no one ever sets out to be controlled by a substance or a behavior. So many times, Lord, Your children don't realize that addictions can harm all relationships—even their relationship with You. May Your Spirit protect this one You love so much. And, may You guide this one on the right path—away from the things of this world that would enslave and destroy.*

# 6

ANGER

# I HAVE AN ANGER PROBLEM

*Sometimes, I have a pretty short fuse,
and get upset easily. How can I handle anger?*

## THE HEART OF JESUS ANSWERS:

*You have heard that the law of Moses says, "Do not murder. If you commit murder, you are subject to judgment." But I say, if you are angry with someone, you are subject to judgment! If you call someone an idiot, you are in danger of being brought before the high council. And if you curse someone, you are in danger of the fires of hell.*

MATTHEW 5:21-22 NLT

JESUS

~~~~~~~~~~~~

The frustrations of everyday living can sometimes get the better of us, and we let minor disappointments cause major problems. When we let ourselves become overly irritated by the inevitable ups and downs of life, we become overstressed, overheated, over-anxious, and just plain angry.

When you let yourself become angry, you are certain to defeat at least one person: yourself. When you let the minor frustrations of everyday life hijack your emotions, you harm yourself and your loved ones. So guard against the kind of angry thinking that takes a toll on your emotions and your relationships. Don't let feelings of anger or frustration rule your life, or, for that matter, your day—your life is simply too short for that, and you deserve much better treatment than that . . . from yourself.

Angry words are dangerous to your emotional and spiritual health. So treat anger as an uninvited guest, and usher it away as quickly—and as quietly—as possible.

———⟨⟩———

**Anger is the noise of the soul;**
**the unseen irritant of the heart;**
**the relentless invader of silence.**

MAX LUCADO

———⟨⟩———

## THE HEART OF JESUS PRAYS:

*Father so many things can lead to anger in a person's life—exhaustion, a sense of being overwhelmed, bitterness, confusion, and so much more. Show Your child how to overcome anger and how to deal with any underlying issues. Let this dear one bring all pain and all problems to You.*

7

ASKING GOD

# I SOMETIMES FEEL GUILTY ASKING GOD FOR THINGS

*Should I be afraid to ask God for the things I really want?*

## THE HEART OF JESUS ANSWERS:

*So I say to you, ask, and it will be given to you; seek, and you will find; knock, and it will be opened to you. For everyone who asks receives, and he who seeks finds, and to him who knocks it will be opened.*

LUKE 11:9-10 NKJV

JESUS

J esus repeatedly encouraged His disciples to petition God to meet their needs. So should we. Genuine, heartfelt prayer causes powerful changes in us and in our world. When we lift our hearts and desires to God, we open ourselves to a never-ending source of divine wisdom and infinite love.

Do you have questions about your future that you can't answer? Do you have needs that you can't meet by yourself? Do you sincerely want to know God's purpose for your life? If so, ask Him for direction, for protection, and for strength—and then keep asking Him every day. Whatever your need, no matter how great or small, pray about it and never lose hope. God is not just near; He is here, and He's perfectly able to answer your prayers. Now, it's just up to you to ask.

If you need something, ask your heavenly Father. And remember: God is listening. In fact, He wants to hear from you right now.

———

When will we realize that we're not troubling
God with our questions and concerns?
His heart is open to hear us—his touch nearer
than our next thought—as if no one in the world
existed but us. Our very personal God
wants to hear from us personally.

GIGI GRAHAM TCHIVIDJIAN

———

## THE HEART OF JESUS PRAYS:

*Father, sometimes Your children are afraid to ask because they think they're presuming, or because they're afraid You'll say "no." May Your Spirit give Your child the courage and confidence to come to You about any needs and ask You about any questions. May Your child learn that You're a God who loves to say "Yes!"*

8

ATTITUDE

# I STRUGGLE
# WITH MY ATTITUDE

*What kind of attitude is best for me
and my friends to have?*

## THE HEART OF JESUS ANSWERS:

*I've told you these things for a purpose: that my joy might be your joy, and your joy wholly mature.*

JOHN 15:11 MSG

JESUS

---

What's your attitude today? Are you afraid, angry, bored, or worried? Are you concerned more about pleasing your friends than about pleasing God? Are you confused, bitter, or pessimistic? If so, God wants to have a little talk with you.

God created you in His own image, and He wants you to experience joy and abundance. But, God will not force His joy upon you; you must be willing to claim it for yourself—you have to choose to be joyful no matter what happens. So today, and every day hereafter, celebrate this life that God has given you. Think optimistically about yourself and your future because God has a great life planned for you! Give thanks to the One who has given you everything, and trust in your heart that He wants to give you so much more.

Jesus came so you might have an attitude of joy. So, please be joyful as you celebrate your temporary life here on earth and your eternal life in heaven.

---

**The people whom I have seen succeed best in life have always been cheerful and hopeful people who went about their business with a smile on their faces.**

CHARLES KINGSLEY

---

## THE HEART OF JESUS PRAYS:

*Father, today as Your child considers the way he or she thinks and behaves, may Your Spirit remind this one that battles are often won or lost in the mind. May Your Spirit prompt this beloved child to think of You every day, and even many times during the day, so that this dear one's mind can reflect Your mind.*

9

# SOME OF MY HABITS ARE SINFUL

*Does God really care about the way we act?*

## THE HEART OF JESUS ANSWERS:

*Blessed are those who hunger and thirst for righteousness, for they will be filled.*

MATTHEW 5:6 NIV

JESUS

---

Life is a series of choices. Each day, we make countless decisions that can bring us closer to God... or farther from Him. When we live according to God's commandments, we enjoy the abundance and peace He intends for our lives. But when we turn our backs on God by ignoring Him—or by disobeying Him—we bring needless pain and suffering upon ourselves and our families.

Do you want God's peace and His blessings? Then obey Him. When you face difficult choices or temptations, seek God's counsel and then trust and follow the counsel He gives. Invite God into your heart and live according to His commandments. When God speaks to you through that little quiet voice that He has placed in your heart, listen. When you do, you will be blessed today, and tomorrow, and forever. And you'll discover that happiness means living according to your beliefs. No exceptions.

How can you guard your steps? By walking with Jesus every day of your life.

———⟨◦⟩———

**Christians are the citizens of heaven,
and while we are on earth,
we ought to behave like heaven's citizens.**
WARREN WIERSBE

———⟨◦⟩———

## THE HEART OF JESUS PRAYS:

*Father, when Your children ask You to be in their lives, You go with them wherever they go. Today, may Your Spirit impress that truth on this one's heart. May this beloved child realize You accompany him or her everywhere not to police what this one does, but because You love Your children so much that You want to be with them. May Your Spirit's presence help this one always choose to walk in the right places and do the right things.*

# 10

# A BOOK UNLIKE
# ANY OTHER

*Is the Bible really God's Word,*
*or is it simply another book?*

## THE HEART OF JESUS ANSWERS:

*Man shall not live by bread alone, but by every word that proceeds from the mouth of God.*

MATTHEW 4:4 NKJV

JESUS

---

The words of Matthew 4:4 remind us that, as believers, we must study the Bible and meditate on its meaning for our lives. Otherwise, we miss out on a priceless gift from our Creator.

God's Word is not like any other book. The Bible is a roadmap for life here on earth and for life eternal. As Christians, we are called upon to study God's Holy Word, to follow its commandments, and to share its Good News with the world.

Jonathan Edwards advised, "Be assiduous in reading the Holy Scriptures. This is the fountain whence all knowledge in divinity must be derived. Therefore let not this treasure lie by you neglected." God's Holy Word is truly a priceless, one-of-a-kind treasure. It's not enough for Christians to seek to obey God's Word and to understand His will to have only a passing acquaintance with the Good Book. After all, man does not live by bread alone . . .

God intends for you to use His Word as your guide-book for life . . . your intentions should be the same as His.

———⟡———

**Nobody ever outgrows Scripture;
the book widens and deepens with our years.**
C. H. SPURGEON

———⟡———

## THE HEART OF JESUS PRAYS:

*Father, so many times your children wish they could hear directly from You what they should think and do and how they should handle certain situations. May Your Spirit remind them that this is why they have the Bible—as Your love letter and operating manual for how to successfully walk the Christian life. May Your Spirit help them be drawn into the pages and know You better.*

# 11

# HOW DO I OVERCOME BITTERNESS?

*Sometimes I'm bitter about the past.*
*How can I let go of the pain?*

## THE HEART OF JESUS ANSWERS:

*Whenever you stand praying, forgive, if you have anything against anyone, so that your Father in heaven will also forgive you your transgressions.*

MARK 11:25 NASB

JESUS

Bitterness is a spiritual sickness. It will consume your soul and is dangerous to your emotional health. It can destroy you if you let it . . . so don't let it!

If you are caught up in intense feelings of anger or resentment, you know the destructive power of these emotions. How can you rid yourself of these feelings? First, prayerfully ask God to cleanse your heart. Then, learn to catch yourself whenever thoughts of bitterness or hatred begin to attack you. Your big challenge is that you must learn to resist negative thoughts before they hijack your emotions.

Matthew 5:22 teaches us that if we judge our brothers and sisters, we, too, will be subject to judgment. So let's work hard not to judge our neighbors. Instead, let's forgive them and love them—while leaving their judgment to a far more capable authority: the One who sits on His throne in heaven.

Bitterness is both dangerous and self-destructive. Since you can never fully enjoy today if you're bitter about yesterday, make peace with your past now, and move on.

---

**Bitterness is the greatest barrier
to friendship with God.**

RICK WARREN

---

## THE HEART OF JESUS PRAYS:

*Father, sometimes Your children expect so much out of each other. Sometimes they forget that everyone else they meet on earth is only human. May Your Spirit remind them that humans make mistakes and sometimes act in ungodly ways. And may You be with this one who is disappointed. Help this one turn the pain over to You and find Your strength to forgive.*

# 12

BUSYNESS

# I'M ALWAYS BUSY, BUT I CAN'T GET EVERYTHING DONE

*I'm really busy. Isn't that a good thing?*

## THE HEART OF JESUS ANSWERS:

*You're tied down to the mundane; I'm in touch with what is beyond your horizons. You live in terms of what you see and touch. I'm living on other terms. I told you that you were missing God in all this. You're at a dead end. If you won't believe I am who I say I am, you're at the dead end of sins. You're missing God in your lives.*

JOHN 8:23-24 MSG

JESUS

---

Are you making time each day to praise God and to study His Word? If so, you know from experience the blessings He offers those who worship Him consistently and sincerely. But, if you have unintentionally let the hustle and bustle of your busy day come between you and your Creator, then slow down, take a deep breath, and rearrange your priorities!

God loved this world so much that He sent His Son to save it. And now only one real question remains for you: how will you respond to God's love? The answer should be obvious: God must come first in your life. He is the giver of all good things, and He is the One who sent His Son so you could have eternal life. He deserves your prayers, your obedience, your stewardship, and your love—and He deserves these things all day every day, not just on Sunday mornings.

Do first things first, and keep your focus on high-priority tasks. And please remember this: your highest priority should be your relationship with God.

———

**You're busy with all the pressures of the world around you, but in that busyness you're missing the most important element of all— God's ongoing presence that is available to you.**

BILL HYBELS

———

## THE HEART OF JESUS PRAYS:

*Father so many of Your children believe the busier they are, the more productive they are, and as a result, the more worthwhile or important they are. They so easily get caught up in the tyranny of urgency. Help Your children to slow down. Help them learn to take a deep breath and spend a few moments with You, even amid the hecticness of their lives. May Your Spirit teach them that importance doesn't come with how much they do, but how well they do the tasks You assign.*

# 13

# CELEBRATE LIFE!

*Sometimes life is so ho-hum.*
*Why should I be excited about life?*

## THE HEART OF JESUS ANSWERS:

*The master was full of praise. "Well done, my good and faithful servant. You have been faithful in handling this small amount, so now I will give you many more responsibilities. Let's celebrate together!"*

MATTHEW 25:21 NLT

JESUS

———————— ✦ ————————

What is the best day to celebrate life? This one! Today and every day should be filled with prayer and celebration as we consider the Good News of God's free gift: salvation through Jesus Christ.

What do you expect from the day ahead? Are you expecting God to do wonderful things, or are you living beneath a cloud of apprehension and doubt? The words of Psalm 118:24 remind us of a profound but simple truth: "This is the day which the LORD hath made" (KJV). Our duty, as believers, is to rejoice in God's marvelous creation.

For Christians, every day begins and ends with God and His Son. Christ came to this earth to give us abundant life and eternal salvation. We give thanks to our Maker when we treasure each day. May we use our time on earth to serve God, to celebrate His marvelous gifts, and to share His Good News with the world.

Today is a cause for celebration. Please plan your day—and your life—accordingly.

---

**Christ is the secret, the source,
the substance, the center, and the circumference
of all true and lasting gladness.**

MRS. CHARLES E. COWMAN

---

## THE HEART OF JESUS PRAYS:

*Father help your children to rejoice and realize that they've received one of the most priceless gifts You can give them: the gift of life! May Your Spirit help them remember that they're on the earth for a reason, for a joyous reason. And that they fill a role that only they can do in the great scheme of Your kingdom.*

14

CHANGE

# ALWAYS CHANGING

*My world is changing faster and faster.*
*Shouldn't I be concerned?*

## THE HEART OF JESUS ANSWERS:

*Therefore do not worry about tomorrow, for tomorrow will worry about itself. Each day has enough trouble of its own.*

MATTHEW 6:34 NIV

JESUS

e live in a world that is always moving and adjusting, but we worship a God who will never change—thank goodness! That means we can be comforted in the knowledge that our Heavenly Father is the rock that simply cannot be moved: "I am the Lord, I do not change" (Malachi 3:6 NKJV).

The next time you face difficult circumstances, tough times, unfair treatment, or unwelcome changes, remember that some things are never different—things like the love that you feel in your heart for your family and friends . . . and the love that God feels for you. So instead of worrying too much about life's inevitable challenges, focus your energies on finding solutions. Have faith in your own abilities, do your best to solve your problems as you feel God is guiding you, and leave the rest up to God.

The world changes, but I don't. So, please don't worry. The tough times you experience today will pale in comparison to the joys you'll experience in heaven.

⸻

**I can't do much about changing the world, but I can do something about bringing God's presence into the world in which He has put me.**

WARREN WIERSBE

⸻

## THE HEART OF JESUS PRAYS:

*Father, some of Your children handle change better than others. To some, change is exciting, like a roller-coaster ride. Others are more comfortable with routine. Help your children remember that You know exactly how much excitement each of Your children can handle and may Your Spirit reassure them that You will never allow them to face more than they can handle.*

# 15

# HOW DO I CHOOSE MORE WISELY?

*I have lots of choices every day.*
*How do I know if I'm making the decisions*
*God wants me to?*

## THE HEART OF JESUS ANSWERS:

*The thing you should want most is God's kingdom and doing what God wants. Then all these other things you need will be given to you.*

MATTHEW 6:33 NCV

JESUS

---

From the instant you wake up in the morning until the moment you nod off to sleep at night, you make countless decisions—decisions about the things you do, decisions about the words you speak, and decisions about the way you direct your thoughts.

As a believer who has been transformed by the radical love of Jesus, you have every reason to make wise choices. But sometimes, when the daily grind threatens to chew you up and spit you out, you may make choices that displease God.

As you consider the kind of Christian you are—and the kind of Christian you want to become—ask yourself whether you're sitting on the fence between the world and God's world, or standing in the light of God's presence. And while you're at it, ask yourself if you're choosing friends who help you make smart decisions, not dumb ones. Remember: if you sincerely want to follow the footsteps of the One from Galilee, make choices that are pleasing to Him. He deserves no less . . . and neither do you.

Choices have consequences. The quality of your choices will determine the direction and the quality of your life. When you face an important decision, ask for God's guidance.

Life is a series of choices between
the bad, the good, and the best.
Everything depends on how we choose.

VANCE HAVNER

## THE HEART OF JESUS PRAYS:

*Father the enemy is the author of confusion, an enemy who takes joy in pushing Your beloved children into making bad choices. May Your Spirit so fill this believer's life that this one hears Your voice clearly and strongly. May the voice of the enemy become a whisper compared to the joyous shout You provide.*

# 16

---

# I DON'T FEEL LOVED

---

*I know Jesus loves me.*
*But what does that really mean in everyday life?*

## THE HEART OF JESUS ANSWERS:

*As the Father hath loved me, so have I loved you; continue ye in my love.*

JOHN 15:9 KJV

JESUS

❦

How much does Christ love us? More than we, mere mortals, can comprehend. His love is perfect and steadfast. Even though we make mistakes and are wayward, the Good Shepherd still cares for us. Even when we have fallen far short of the Father's commandments, Christ loves us with a power and depth beyond our understanding. The sacrifice that Jesus made on the cross was made for each of us, and His love endures to the edge of eternity and beyond.

Christ's love changes everything. When you accept His gift of grace, you are transformed, for today and for all eternity. If you haven't already done so, accept Jesus Christ as your Savior. He's waiting patiently for you to invite Him into your heart. Don't make Him wait a single minute longer!

Jesus loves you. And, He wants you to be with Him today, tomorrow, and forever.

Live your lives in love, the same
sort of love which Christ gives us,
and which He perfectly expressed
when He gave Himself
as a sacrifice to God.

—

CORRIE TEN BOOM

⸺⸺

## THE HEART OF JESUS PRAYS:

*Father, it's so hard for Your children to understand the love that I have for them and that You have for them. May Your Spirit gently, constantly whisper into their hearts how much they are treasured. May this one know that it takes an amazing amount of love to die for someone else.*

# 17

COMPLAINING

# IS IT WRONG TO COMPLAIN?

*Sometimes, I'm tempted to complain.
That's not really a big deal, is it?*

## THE HEART OF JESUS ANSWERS:

*I've told you these things for a purpose: that my joy might be your joy, and your joy wholly mature.*

JOHN 15:11 MSG

JESUS

Most of us have more blessings than we can count, yet we can still find reasons to complain about the minor frustrations of everyday life. To do so, of course, is not only shortsighted, but it is also a serious roadblock on the path to spiritual abundance.

Would you like to feel more comfortable about your circumstances and your life? Then promise yourself that you'll do whatever it takes to focus your thoughts and energy on the major blessings you've received (not on the minor inconveniences you must occasionally endure).

So the next time you're tempted to complain about the inevitable frustrations of everyday living, don't! Today and every day, make it a practice to count your blessings, not your hardships. It's the truly decent way to live.

Jesus wants you to experience joyful abundance, and complaining gets in the way. So the next time you're tempted to complain, count your blessings, not your hardships.

---

**Jesus wept, but he never complained.**

C. H. SPURGEON

---

## THE HEART OF JESUS PRAYS:

*Father, it's so easy for Your people living on earth to look at the negative side of life and talk about the bad things or the things they perceive as bad. Send Your Spirit to fill them with the knowledge that You allow everything that comes into their lives for a reason. Help them to focus on looking for that reason. Instead of spending their energy talking about the challenges, may Your Spirit help them look for Your solutions.*

# 18

---

# I NEED MORE CONFIDENCE

---

*Sometimes, I feel a lack of confidence.*
*What should I do?*

## THE HEART OF JESUS ANSWERS:

*I've told you all this so that trusting me, you will be unshakable and assured, deeply at peace. In this godless world you will continue to experience difficulties. But take heart! I've conquered the world.*

JOHN 16:33 MSG

JESUS

---

We have many reasons to be confident. God is in His heaven; Christ has risen, and we are the sheep of His flock. Yet sometimes, even the most devout Christians can become discouraged. Discouragement, however, is not God's way; He is a God of possibility not negativity.

God is never distant, and He never stops caring about you. He is with you every minute of every day. He hears your every prayer and knows your every thought. When times are good, He rejoices with you. When times are tough, God's got your back.

Are you a confident Christian? You should be. God's grace is eternal and His promises are unambiguous. So count your blessings, not your hardships. And live courageously. God is the Giver of all things good, and He watches over you today and forever.

Please don't be afraid. Because God is with you always, you can live confidently.

—⊰⊱—

**Believe and do what God says.**
**The life-changing consequences will be limitless,**
**and the results will be confidence**
**and peace of mind.**
FRANKLIN GRAHAM

—⊰⊱—

## THE HEART OF JESUS PRAYS:

*Father, help this child of Yours learn to see more with a heart of faith and with spiritual eyes. Help this one feel an awareness of Your presence in every area of life so that this child You love can confidently know You're always on duty to protect, guard, and guide.*

# 19

---

CONSCIENCE

# THAT VOICE INSIDE

---

*Something inside tells me one thing,*
*so why am I tempted to do the opposite?*

## THE HEART OF JESUS ANSWERS:

*But seek first the kingdom of God and His righteousness, and all these things shall be added to you.*

MATTHEW 6:33 NKJV

JESUS

G od gave you a conscience for a very good reason: as a tool to help your path conform to His will. Billy Graham correctly observed, "Most of us follow our conscience as we follow a wheelbarrow. We push it in front of us in the direction we want to go." To try to change the direction our conscience is telling us to go is a big mistake. Yet all of us have occasionally failed to listen to the voice God planted in our hearts. And all of us have suffered the negative consequences.

Wise believers make it a practice to listen carefully to that quiet internal voice. Count yourself among that number. When your conscience speaks, listen, and learn. In all likelihood, God is trying to get His message through. And in all likelihood, it is a message you desperately need to hear.

God gave you a conscience for a very good reason: to use it. Treat your conscience as you would a trusted advisor. In every situation, and in every circumstance, let your conscience be your guide. God will never lead you astray. Never.

---

**It is neither safe nor prudent
to do anything against one's conscience.**
MARTIN LUTHER

---

## THE HEART OF JESUS PRAYS:

*Father, when You created each person, You put a special little part of Yourself inside of them—their conscience. Help this child You love so much learn to trust that little voice as an indication of Your presence, and of Your love.*

# 20

CONTENTMENT

# WHAT IS THE SECRET OF CONTENTMENT?

*At times, I feel discontented with life.*
*How can I find lasting peace?*

## THE HEART OF JESUS ANSWERS:

*You're blessed when you're content with just who you are—*
*no more, no less. That's the moment you find yourselves*
*proud owners of everything that can't be bought.*

MATTHEW 5:5 MSG

JESUS

---

W here can you find contentment? Does satisfaction in life come with wealth or power or beauty or fame? Hardly. Genuine contentment springs from a peaceful spirit, a clear conscience, and a loving heart (like yours!).

People in the world seem preoccupied with the search for happiness. We are bombarded with messages telling us that happiness depends upon the way we look or the things we own. These messages are false. Lasting contentment cannot be bought; it must be earned through healthy thoughts, sincere prayers, and good behavior. And if we don't find contentment within ourselves, we will never find it outside ourselves.

So the search for contentment is an internal quest, an exploration of the heart, mind, and soul. You can find contentment—indeed you will find it—if you simply look in the right places. And the best time to start looking in those places is now.

Are you a contented Christian? If your spirit is temporarily troubled, perhaps you need to focus less on your own priorities and more on God's priorities. When you do, you'll rediscover this life-changing truth: Genuine contentment begins with God . . . and ends there.

———

**Contentment is something we learn by adhering to the basics—cultivating a growing relationship with Jesus Christ, living daily, and knowing that Christ strengthens us for every challenge.**

CHARLES STANLEY

———

## THE HEART OF JESUS PRAYS:

*Father, so many of Your children don't realize that the search for peace and contentment in their life is not emotional, but spiritual. It's really an indication of their souls longing to draw closer to You. Be with this one today and draw their heart near You. May this one find the comfort of nestling within Your presence.*

# 21

CONVERSION

# THE BRAND NEW YOU!

*What does the Bible say about
becoming a new creation?*

## THE HEART OF JESUS ANSWERS:

*Then He called a child to Him and had him stand among them. "I assure you," He said, "unless you are converted and become like children, you will never enter the kingdom of heaven."*

MATTHEW 18:2-3 HCSB

JESUS

---

Think, for a moment, about the "old" you, the person you were before you invited Christ to reign over your heart. Now, think about the "new" you, the person you have become since then. Is there a difference between the "old" you and the "new and improved" version? There should be! And not only should you notice that difference, but others should, too!

The Bible clearly teaches that when we welcome Christ into our hearts, we become new creations through Him. Our challenge, of course, is to act like new creations—in our words, actions, and thoughts. When we do, God fills our hearts, He blesses our endeavors, and He transforms our lives . . . forever.

Jesus is ready to revolutionize your life today. He's standing at the door of your heart, waiting patiently.

Turn your life over to Him, and let Him do the rest. When you follow in His footsteps, you'll be protected today; you'll be protected tomorrow, and you'll be protected for all eternity.

---

**Being a Christian is more than just
an instantaneous conversion;
it is like a daily process whereby you grow
to be more and more like Christ.**

BILLY GRAHAM

---

## THE HEART OF JESUS PRAYS:

*Father, I ask You to help Your children awaken to the realization that they are never the same after they have turned their lives over to You. Give this one we love a deep sense of the ways that Your Spirit infuses new life, new hope, and new direction!*

# 22

COURAGE

# I WOULD LIKE TO BE COURAGEOUS

*Sometimes life is downright scary.*
*When I'm afraid, what should I do?*

## THE HEART OF JESUS ANSWERS:

*But He said to them, "Why are you fearful, you of little faith?" Then He got up and rebuked the winds and the sea. And there was a great calm.*

MATTHEW 8:26 HCSB

JESUS

---

A storm rose quickly on the Sea of Galilee while the disciples were in a boat that was not made to withstand severe storms. The fierceness of the storm was enough to rattle these men, including the ones who were fishermen and used to rough seas. Although they had seen Jesus perform many miracles, the disciples still feared for their lives. In their fear, they did the wisest thing imaginable—they turned to their Savior, and He calmed the waters and the wind.

Sometimes, we, like the disciples, feel threatened by the storms of life. And when we are fearful, we, too, can turn to Christ for courage and for comfort.

From time to time, all of us, even the most devout believers, experience fear. But, as believers, we can live courageously in the promises of our Lord . . . and we should.

As you take the next step on your life's journey, feel reassured: Wherever you find yourself, God is there. And, because He cares for you, you can live courageously.

Because of Me, you have every reason on earth—and in heaven—to live courageously. And that's exactly what you should do.

~~~~~

**The truth of Christ brings assurance and so removes the former problem of fear and uncertainty.**

A. W. TOZER

~~~~~

## THE HEART OF JESUS PRAYS:

*Father, the human heart and spirit is so fragile. It's so easy for these children of Yours to be frightened by their lack of control. Please send Your Spirit deep into their hearts and lives to remind them that they don't have to be in charge because You're already on duty. Teach them that real courage is trusting You to handle the problems that are simply too big for them to solve.*

# 23

DAILY DEVOTIONAL

# EVERY DAY WITH GOD

*I can't always find time to study my Bible
every day. Is that really such a big deal?*

## THE HEART OF JESUS ANSWERS:

*If anyone wants to come with Me, he must deny himself, take up his cross daily, and follow Me.*

LUKE 9:23 HCSB

JESUS

---

When it comes to spending time with God, are you a "squeezer" or a "pleaser"? Do you squeeze God into your schedule with a prayer before meals (and maybe, if you've got the time, with a quick visit to church on Sunday)? Or do you please God by talking to Him far more than that and reading His word? The answer to this question will determine the direction of your day and the quality of your life.

Each day has 1,440 minutes—do you value your relationship with God enough to spend a few of those minutes with Him? Hopefully so. But if you find that you're simply "too busy" for a daily chat with your Father in heaven, take a long, hard look at your priorities and your values.

Warren Wiersbe writes, "Surrender your mind to the Lord at the beginning of each day." That's sound advice.

So, if you've acquired the unfortunate habit of trying to squeeze God into the corners of your life, reshuffle the items on your to-do list by placing God first. God wants your undivided attention—not the leftovers of your day. And if you haven't already done so, form the habit of spending quality time with your Father in heaven. He deserves it . . . and so do you.

---

Make a plan now to keep a daily appointment
with God. The enemy is going to tell you
to set it aside, but you must carve out the time.
If you're too busy to meet with the Lord,
friend, then you are simply too busy.

CHARLES SWINDOLL

---

## THE HEART OF JESUS PRAYS:

*Father, human leaders have pointed out that to fail to plan is to plan to fail. Help this child You love not only see the value in spending time with You, but to long to meet with You. Make the desire so strong that planning time with You is as exciting and joyful as if Your child were planning a date with a new love interest. Help this one You love overcome the obstacles to meet with You regularly.*

# 24

---

# WHY ARE PEOPLE SO DIFFICULT?

*Some people are just hard to get along with.
How should I deal with those people?*

## THE HEART OF JESUS ANSWERS:

*But when you are praying, first forgive anyone you are holding a grudge against, so that your Father in heaven will forgive your sins, too.*

MARK 11:25 NLT

JESUS

Sometimes people can be difficult . . . very difficult. And when they are, we may be tempted to strike back, either verbally or in some other way. But usually, there's a better way—our job is to find it.

Susan L. Taylor correctly observed, "Not everybody is healthy enough to have a front-row seat in your life." In other words, the best way to deal with some aggravating people is to distance yourself from them.

As long as you live on Planet Earth, you'll face countless opportunities to lose your temper when other folks behave badly. But God has a better plan: He wants you to forgive and move on. And He wants you to do it now.

Until you learn how to forgive, you're locked inside a prison of your own making. Forgiveness is its own reward and bitterness is its own punishment. Guard your words and your thoughts accordingly.

You can be sure you are abiding
in Christ if you are able to have
a Christlike love toward
the people that irritate you the most.

—

VONETTE BRIGHT

## THE HEART OF JESUS PRAYS:

*Father, help this child of Yours to always try to show love and respect, remembering that the people who hurt us and may appear to be annoying are also ones You love and I died to redeem. Help this one know when to keep showing Your love, and when to gently walk away and let us deal with that person. I also ask that You fill this child with such a great sense of Your love that it spills over onto others—even those who are difficult.*

# 25

---

# DARE TO FOLLOW

---

*What do I need to know about being
a disciple of Jesus in today's world?*

## THE HEART OF JESUS ANSWERS:

*You did not choose Me, but I chose you. I appointed you that you should go out and produce fruit, and that your fruit should remain, so that whatever you ask the Father in My name, He will give you.*

JOHN 15:16 HCSB

JESUS

---

The 19th-century writer Hannah Whitall Smith observed, "The crucial question for each of us is this: What do you think of Jesus, and do you yet have a personal acquaintance with Him?" The answer to that question will determine the quality, the course, and the direction of your life today and for all eternity.

Jesus has called believers of every generation (and that includes you) to walk with Him. Jesus promises that when you follow in His footsteps, He will teach you how to live freely and lightly (Matthew 11:28-30). When Jesus makes a promise, you can depend upon it.

Are you worried or anxious about what it means to walk as Christ's disciple, or about any other area of life? Be confident in the power of Christ. He will never desert you. Are you discouraged? Be courageous and call upon your Savior. He will protect you and use you according to His purposes. Do you seek to be a worthy disciple of the One from Galilee? Then pick up His cross today and every day of your life. When you do, He will bless you now . . . and forever.

---

**It is the secret of true discipleship to bear the cross,
to acknowledge the death sentence that
has been passed on self, and to deny any right
that self has to rule over us.**

ANDREW MURRAY

---

## THE HEART OF JESUS PRAYS:

*Father, we know that following Me often involves a cost for Your beloved children living on earth. And sometimes that cost can make these dear children hesitate. Move Your spirit into this dear one to show that following in My footsteps and walking with Us brings so much more joy than sorrow. Help our dear one know any cost is light compared with the incredible benefits of discipleship!*

# 26

DOUBTS

# I HAVE DOUBTS

*Sometimes I have doubts about my future and*
*doubts about my faith. What should I do?*

## THE HEART OF JESUS ANSWERS:

*Let not your heart be troubled: ye believe in God, believe also in me.*

JOHN 14:1 KJV

JESUS

⁓⧫⁓

Have you ever wondered if God hears your prayers? If so, you're not the first person to have these questions. Doubts come in many shapes and sizes: doubts about God, doubts about the future, and doubts about your own abilities, just for starters. And what, precisely, does God's Word say in response to these doubts? The Bible is clear: when you are overwhelmed with doubts, of whatever kind, draw nearer to God through worship and prayer. When you do, God, the loving Father who has never left your side, draws ever closer to you (James 4:8).

Is prayer an integral part of your daily life, or is it an inconsistent habit? Do you "pray without ceasing," or is prayer as an afterthought? If your prayer life leaves something to be desired, you rob yourself of a deeper and more personal relationship with God. And how can you rectify that situation? By praying more frequently and more fervently.

The quality of your spiritual life will be in direct proportion to the quality of your prayer life: the more you pray, the closer you will feel to God. So today, instead of turning things over in your mind, turn them over to God in prayer. Instead of worrying about your next decision, ask God to lead the way. Don't limit your prayers to the dinner table or your bedtime. Pray constantly about things great and small. When you do, your Heavenly Father will take care of you . . . and your doubts will take care of themselves.

---

**Doubting may temporarily disturb, but will not permanently destroy, your faith in Christ.**

CHARLES SWINDOLL

---

## THE HEART OF JESUS PRAYS:

*Father, You and I both understand the human tendency to doubt, especially since they have seen so much in their world not be what they were led to believe it would be. Help this dear child of Yours stay strong and feel a sense of Your presence. Help this dear one believe in Your promises, no matter what appearances may be or what the enemy may whisper.*

27

DREAMS

# I'M AFRAID
# MY DREAMS WON'T
# EVER COME TRUE

*I have big dreams.*
*How do I know if they're from God?*

## THE HEART OF JESUS ANSWERS:

*I came so they can have real and eternal life, more and better life than they ever dreamed of.*

JOHN 10:10 MSG

JESUS

---

How big are you willing to dream? Are you willing to entertain the possibility that God has big plans in store for you? Or are you convinced that your future is so dim you'd better wear night goggles? Well here are the facts: if you're a believer in the One from Galilee, you have an incredibly bright future ahead of you . . . here on earth and in heaven. That's why you have every right to dream big.

Concentration camp survivor, Corrie ten Boom observed, "Every experience God gives us, every person he brings into our lives, is the perfect preparation for the future that only he can see." These words apply to you.

It takes courage to dream big dreams. You will discover that courage when you do three things: accept the past, trust God to handle the future, and make the most of the time He has given you today.

Nothing is too difficult for God, and no dreams are too big for Him—not even yours. So start living—and dreaming—accordingly.

Trust God, trust Christ, and believe in yourself. You can do big things if you believe.

---

**Set goals so big that unless God helps you, you will be a miserable failure.**

BILL BRIGHT

---

## THE HEART OF JESUS PRAYS:

*Father, how exciting it is when one of Your children gets a glimpse of how he or she can change the world through Your strength and power. And how thrilling when our humans dare to believe Your calling and mission for them. Help this dear child recall the stories in Your Word about the ones who dared dream big for You: Joseph, David, Peter, Esther, and so many others. Help this one see how you use ordinary people in extraordinary ways!*

# 28

---

## DUTIES

# I HAVE SO MUCH TO DO, BUT I'M NOT SURE WHAT TO DO FIRST

*I have lots of responsibilities.*
*What's the godly way to handle them?*

## THE HEART OF JESUS ANSWERS:

*For everyone who practices wicked things hates the light and avoids it, so that his deeds may not be exposed. But anyone who lives by the truth comes to the light, so that his works may be shown to be accomplished by God.*

JOHN 3:20-21 HCSB

JESUS

---

Nobody needs to tell you the obvious: You have lots of responsibilities—obligations to yourself, to your family, to your community, and to your God. Which of these duties should take priority? You can find the answer in Matthew 6:33: "But seek first the kingdom of God and His righteousness, and all these things will be provided for you" (HCSB).

When you "seek first the kingdom of God," all your other obligations have a way of falling into place. When you obey God's Word and seek His will, your many responsibilities don't seem like such a burden. When you honor God with your time, your talents. and your prayers, you're much more likely to count your blessings instead of your troubles.

Do yourself and your loved ones a favor: take all your duties seriously, especially your duties to God.

When you do, you'll discover that pleasing your Father in heaven isn't just the right thing to do; it's also the best way to live.

Follow Jesus and fulfill your responsibilities. When you accept your duties and fulfill them, you'll feel good about yourself. When you avoid your obligations, you won't.

⁂

**If you seek to know the path of your duty, use God as your compass.**

C. H. SPURGEON

⁂

## THE HEART OF JESUS PRAYS:

*Father, help this one we love remember that he or she is so important as Your ambassador on earth. Remind this one that the responsibilities Your children bear are often Your way of partnering with Your children to see Your will done on earth.*

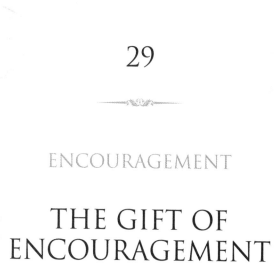

29

ENCOURAGEMENT

# THE GIFT OF
# ENCOURAGEMENT

*So many people around me seem to need*
*encouragement. What should I do?*

## THE HEART OF JESUS ANSWERS:

*I tell you the truth, anything you did for even the least of my people here, you also did for me.*

MATTHEW 25:40 NCV

JESUS

---

L ife is a team sport, and all of us need occasional pats on the back from our teammates. As Christians, we are called upon to spread the Good News of Christ, and we are also called to spread a message of encouragement and hope to the world.

Whether you realize it or not, many people you come in contact with every day desperately need a smile or an encouraging word. The world can be a difficult place, and friends and family members may be troubled by the challenges of everyday life. Since we don't always know who needs our help, the best strategy is to try to encourage all the people who cross our paths. So today, be a world-class source of encouragement to everyone you meet. Never has the need been greater.

Jesus wants you to feed His sheep and encourage His children. You can't lift other people up without lifting yourself up, too.

God is still in the process
of dispensing gifts,
and He uses ordinary individuals
like us to develop those gifts
in other people.

HOWARD HENDRICKS

## THE HEART OF JESUS PRAYS:

*Father, help this dear one remember that when Your children on earth give Your wisdom and encouragement to others, they are being like You, the God of all good and all encouragement—and they are so often the source through which Your Spirit can minister to a discouraged soul. May this child of Yours be given hope and joy even as he or she dispenses it to others.*

## 30

ETERNAL LIFE

# THE LIFE THAT OVERCOMES DEATH

*When I think about death, I'm afraid.*
*Is this normal?*

## THE HEART OF JESUS ANSWERS:

*For what does it benefit a man to gain the whole world yet lose his life? What can a man give in exchange for his life?*

MARK 8:36-37 HCSB

JESUS

---

Your life here on earth is merely a preparation for a far different life to come: the eternal life God promises to those who welcome His Son into their hearts.

As a mortal, your vision for the future is finite. God's vision is not burdened by such limitations: His plans extend throughout all eternity. Because of this, God's plans for you are not limited to the ups and downs of everyday life. Your Heavenly Father has bigger things in mind . . . much bigger things.

As you struggle with the inevitable hardships and occasional disappointments of life, remember that God has invited you to accept His abundance not only for today but also for all eternity. So keep things in perspective. Although you will inevitably encounter occasional defeats in this world, you'll have all eternity to celebrate the ultimate victory in the next.

Death is inevitable, but you don't know when it's going to happen. So as you make plans for life here on earth and for life eternal, please accept His invitation of eternal life. Be with Him now and forever.

<hr />

**The believing Christian has hope as he stands at the grave of a loved one who is with the Lord, for he knows that the separation is not forever. It is a glorious truth that those who are in Christ never see each other for the last time.**

BILLY GRAHAM

<hr />

## THE HEART OF JESUS PRAYS:

*Father, humans are somewhat naturally concerned about the unknown. When this dear child fears leaving this world, may Your Spirit comfort and remind this one that I am with each person always, even unto the end of the world. And death is not so much leaving earth as it is the act of finally going home—to the home earth is only a reflection of.*

# 31

---

## EVIL

# DOES EVIL EXIST?

---

*This world can be a crazy place.*
*What should I do about the evils that I encounter?*

## THE HEART OF JESUS ANSWERS:

*Don't fear those who kill the body but are not able to kill the soul; but rather, fear Him who is able to destroy both soul and body in hell.*

MATTHEW 10:28 HCSB

JESUS

---

This world is God's creation, and it contains the wonderful fruits of His handiwork. But the world also contains so many opportunities to stray from God's will. Temptations are everywhere, and the devil, it seems, never takes a day off. Our task, as believers, is to turn away from temptation and to place our lives squarely in the center of God's will.

In his letter to Jewish Christians, Peter offered a stern warning: "Your adversary, the devil, prowls around like a roaring lion, seeking someone to devour" (1 Peter 5:8 NASB). This was true in New Testament times and is equally true in our own. Evil is indeed abroad in the world, and Satan continues to sow the seeds of destruction far and wide. As followers of Christ Jesus, we must guard our hearts by earnestly wrapping ourselves in the protection of God's Holy Word. When we do, we are protected.

There is darkness in this world, but God's light can overpower any darkness. Follow Christ Jesus beyond the darkness.

---

**Christianity isn't a religion about going to Sunday school, potluck suppers, being nice, holding car washes, sending your secondhand clothes off to Mexico— as good as those things might be. This is a world at war.**

JOHN ELDREDGE

---

## THE HEART OF JESUS PRAYS:

*Father, help Your child remember that the enemy never takes a vacation, nor calls a truce. But may Your Spirit also remind Your children of the truth in Your book in 1 John 4:4: "Greater is He that is in you than he that is in the world." And may Your Spirit also reassure this dear one to remember to take a look at the back of Your book and realize We win the battle.*

# 32

FAILURE

# I FEEL LIKE A FAILURE

*Sometimes, despite my best efforts,*
*I am unsuccessful. How can I deal with failure?*

## THE HEART OF JESUS ANSWERS:

*I tell you the truth, you will weep and mourn while the world rejoices. You will grieve, but your grief will turn to joy.*

JOHN 16:20 NIV

JESUS

---

The occasional disappointments and failures of life are inevitable. These setbacks are simply the price we must occasionally pay for our willingness to take risks as we follow our dreams. But even when we encounter bitter disappointments, we must never lose faith.

When we encounter the inevitable difficulties of daily life here on earth, God stands ready to protect us and comfort us. Our responsibility, of course, is to ask Him to be with us and to help us. When we call upon our Heavenly Father in heartfelt prayer, He will answer—in His own time and according to His own plan—and He will heal us emotionally. And, while we are waiting for God's plans to unfold and for His healing touch to restore us, we can be comforted in the knowledge that our Creator can overcome any obstacle, even if we cannot.

In this world, you will have disappointments, and setbacks, and heartbreaks. But don't worry; Jesus has overcome the world.

———

**Failure is one of life's most powerful teachers. How we handle our failures determines whether we're going to simply "get by" in life or "press on."**
BETH MOORE

———

## THE HEART OF JESUS PRAYS:

*Father, when this dear one faces disappointments, You will always provide comfort. May Your Spirit show this one that sometimes failures are actually stepping stones to success. May You comfort this one and whisper words of hope and guidance. And, may Your Spirit help this precious child trust in You and Your goodness, no matter what.*

33

---

FAITH

# I'M NOT SURE I HAVE FAITH IN FAITH

---

*How powerful is faith supposed to be in my life?*

## THE HEART OF JESUS ANSWERS:

*I tell you the truth, if you have faith as small as a mustard seed, you can say to this mountain, "Move from here to there" and it will move. Nothing will be impossible for you.*

MATTHEW 17:20 NIV

JESUS

---

I n the months and years ahead, your faith will be tested many times. Every life—including yours—is a series of successes and failures, celebrations and disappointments, joys and sorrows. Every step of the way, through every triumph and tragedy, God will stand by your side and strengthen you . . . if you have faith in Him. Jesus taught His disciples that if they had faith, they could move mountains. You can too.

If you place your faith, your trust, indeed your life in the hands of Christ Jesus, you'll be amazed at the marvelous things He can do with you and through you. Faith is a willingness to believe in things that you cannot see and to trust things that you do not know.

Today and every day, strengthen your faith through praise, through worship, through Bible study, and through prayer. God has big plans for you, so trust His strategies and strengthen your faith in Him. With God, all things are possible, and He stands ready to help you accomplish miraculous things with your life . . . if you have faith.

With God, all things are possible. If you have faith, you can do more than you think.

---

**There are a lot of things in life that are difficult to understand. Faith allows the soul to go beyond what the eyes can see.**
JOHN MAXWELL

---

## THE HEART OF JESUS PRAYS:

*Father, part of the challenge humans face is that they live in a concrete world. They live by what they see, hear, taste, touch, and smell. They know how to exercise their bodies and minds...but not their spirits and souls. Help this one strengthen the spiritual heart by exercising faith; by believing Your Words and Your guidance, today and every day.*

# 34

FOLLOWING CHRIST

# A DAILY JOURNEY

*What do I need to know about walking with Jesus?*

## THE HEART OF JESUS ANSWERS:

*Then Jesus said to them, "Follow Me, and I will make you become fishers of men." They immediately left their nets and followed Him.*

MARK 1:17-18 NKJV

JESUS

J esus loved you so much that He endured unspeakable humiliation and suffering for you. How will you respond to Christ's sacrifice? Will you follow Him (Luke 9:23), or will you choose another path? When you place your hopes squarely at the foot of the cross, when you place Jesus squarely at the center of your life, you will be blessed.

When Jesus invited His disciples to become "fishers of men," He was speaking only to that tiny band of followers, but also to you. And, He is still speaking to your heart today. At this very moment, the Son of God is calling you to respond to a life-altering invitation. He is inviting you to become His disciple. He is asking you to trust Him and to follow Him.

Christ showed enduring love for all His believers by willingly sacrificing His own life so that we might have eternal life. Now, it is our turn to become His friend.

Jesus invites you to follow in His footsteps. Please welcome Him into your heart today.

———⟨∘⟩———

**A disciple is a follower of Christ.**
**That means you take on His priorities as your own.**
**His agenda becomes your agenda.**
**His mission becomes your mission.**
CHARLES STANLEY

———⟨∘⟩———

## THE HEART OF JESUS PRAYS:

*Father, each of Your children has a missing piece in his or her heart. They try so many different ways to fill this void. Please send Your Spirit to remind them that the hole is God-shaped. Only a relationship with You through Me can fill that friendship void. May Your Spirit draw them to seek a relationship with Us.*

# 35

# FORGIVENESS IS HARD

*Sometimes it's hard for me to forgive*
*the people who have hurt me.*
*What do I need to know about forgiveness?*

## THE HEART OF JESUS ANSWERS:

*If you forgive those who sin against you, your heavenly Father will forgive you. But if you refuse to forgive others, your Father will not forgive your sins.*

MATTHEW 6:14-15 NLT

JESUS

Forgiveness is seldom easy, but it is always right. When we forgive those who have hurt us, we honor God by obeying His commandments. But when we harbor bitterness against others, we disobey God—with predictably unhappy results.

Are you easily frustrated by the inevitable shortcomings of others? Are you a prisoner of bitterness or regret? Do you focus so intently on the past that you lose sight of the very bright future God has in store for you? If so, perhaps you need a refresher course in the art of forgiveness.

If there exists even one person, alive or dead, whom you have not forgiven (and that includes yourself), follow God's commandment and His will for your life: forgive that person today. And remember that bitterness, anger, and regret are not part of God's plan for your life. Forgiveness is.

Since God has forgiven you, you can (and should) forgive everybody. Because it's never too soon, or too late, to forgive, to forget, and to move on with life.

―――――⁂―――――

**Bitterness is the trap that snares the hunter.**
MAX LUCADO

―――――⁂―――――

## THE HEART OF JESUS PRAYS:

*Father, "Forgive them" is sometimes the hardest phrase for Your disciples on earth to utter. Please let Your Spirit remind this beloved child that You are not finished working on anyone who is still on earth. Help this one have patience with others, realizing that Your work in their lives is not finished yet.*

# 36

---

FUTURE

# WHAT DOES MY
# FUTURE HOLD?

---

*Sometimes I'm worried about the future.
How can I keep from letting concern
about the future spoil my life today?*

## THE HEART OF JESUS ANSWERS:

*Be glad and rejoice, because your reward is great in heaven.*

MATTHEW 5:12 HCSB

JESUS

---

Because we are saved by a risen Christ, we can have hope for the future, no matter how troublesome our present circumstances seem. After all, God has promised that we are His throughout eternity. And He has told us that we must place our hopes in Him.

Of course we will face disappointments and failures while we are here on earth, but these are only temporary defeats. This world can be a place of trials and tribulations, but when we place our trust in God, we are secure. He has promised us peace, joy, and eternal life. And God always keeps His promises.

Are you willing to place your future in the hands of a loving and all-knowing God? Do you trust in the ultimate goodness of His plan for your life? Will you face today's challenges with optimism and hope? You should. After all, God created you for a very important purpose: His purpose. And you still have important work to do: His work.

Today, as you live in the present and look to the future, remember that God has a plan for you. Act—and believe—accordingly.

Because of Christ your future is bright. Look for the brightness. And focus more on future opportunities than on past disappointments.

———

**Do not limit the limitless God!
With Him, face the future unafraid
because you are never alone.**
MRS. CHARLES E. COWMAN

———

## THE HEART OF JESUS PRAYS:

*Father, may Your Spirit remind this dear one that it's only natural for humans to fear the unknown. Help this child of Yours remember that just as Your Word tells us in Jeremiah that You had a future and a hope planned for the Israelites, You already have an ultimately-wonderful future planned for this one, too. May this dear child relax because You're a loving Father and the future is in Your hands.*

# 37

GENEROSITY

# THE JOY OF GIVING

*Is generosity an act of faith and godliness—*
*or a personal choice?*

## THE HEART OF JESUS ANSWERS:

*I tell you the truth, whatever you did for one of the least of these brothers of mine, you did for me.*

MATTHEW 25:40 NIV

JESUS

The words are familiar to those who study God's Word: "Freely you have received, freely give." God has given so much to us. In return, we must give freely of our time, our possessions, our testimonies, and our love.

Your salvation was earned at a terrible price: Christ gave His life for you on the cross at Calvary. Christ's gift is priceless, yet when you accept Jesus as your personal Savior, His gift of eternal life costs you nothing. From those to whom much has been given, much is required. And because you have received the gift of salvation, you are now called by God to be a cheerful, generous steward of the gifts He has placed under your care.

Today and every day that follows, let Christ's words guide you and let His eternal love fill your heart. When you do, your stewardship will be a reflection of your love for Him, and that's exactly as it should be. After all, He loved you first.

God has given so much to you, and He wants you to share His gifts with others. The right time to be generous is now.

---

**I can usually sense that a leading is from the Holy Spirit when it calls me to humble myself, to serve somebody, to encourage somebody, or to give something away.**

BILL HYBELS

---

## THE HEART OF JESUS PRAYS:

*Father, today I ask that Your Spirit helps this dear child remember all the gifts and blessings he or she has received from You. May this one overflow with gratitude at what You have done. And from an overflowing heart and a faith that You will always provide, may this one learn the joy of giving— out of love for others and love for You.*

## 38

## GOD'S CALLING

# WHAT DOES GOD
# WANT ME TO DO?

*I'm not sure that I feel "called" by God.
How can I experience that special sense of
His mark on my life?*

## THE HEART OF JESUS ANSWERS:

*So the last shall be first, and the first last: for many be called, but few chosen.*

MATTHEW 20:16 KJV

JESUS

God is calling you to follow a specific path that He has chosen for your life. And it is vitally important that you heed that call. Otherwise, your talents and opportunities may go unused.

Have you already heard God's call? And are you pursuing it with vigor? If so, you're both fortunate and wise. But if you have not yet discovered what God intends for you to do with your life, keep searching and keep praying until you discover why the Creator put you here.

Remember: God has important work for you to do—work that no one else on earth can accomplish but you. The Creator has placed you in a particular location, amid particular people, with unique opportunities to serve. And He has given you all the tools you need to succeed. So listen for His voice, watch for His signs, and prepare yourself for the call that is sure to come.

God calls you to a life that is perfectly suited for you, a life that will bring happiness and satisfaction to yourself and to others. Follow God's calling.

---

**God never calls without enabling us.**
**In other words, if he calls you to do something,**
**he makes it possible for you to do it.**
LUCI SWINDOLL

---

## THE HEART OF JESUS PRAYS:

*Father, help this dear one realize that a calling is not as much an emotion as a choice to obey You. The more Your children walk in the light that You have shed, the more connected to You and secure in Your love they feel. May this dear child realize that to be a Christian means being called to follow and serve You step by step.*

39

# ALLOWING GOD TO GUIDE

*I want God to guide me;
should I do anything to make that happen?*

## THE HEART OF JESUS ANSWERS:

*Look, I am sending you out as sheep among wolves. Be as wary as snakes and harmless as doves.*

MATTHEW 10:16 NLT

JESUS

The Bible promises that God will guide you if you let Him. So your job is to let Him. But sometimes you will be tempted to do otherwise. Sometimes, you'll be tempted to go along with the crowd; other times, you'll be tempted to do things your way, not God's way. When you feel those temptations, resist them.

What will you allow to guide you through the coming day: your own desires (or, for that matter, the desires of your friends)? Or will you allow God to lead the way? The answer should be obvious. You should let God be your guide. When you entrust your life to Him completely and without reservation, God will give you the strength to meet any challenge, the courage to face any trial, and the wisdom to live in His righteousness. So trust Him today and seek His guidance. When you do, your next step will be the right one.

Your Heavenly Father loves you and wants the best for you. Pray for guidance. When you seek it, He will give it.

---

**Enjoy the adventure of receiving God's guidance. Taste it, revel in it, appreciate the fact that the journey is often a lot more exciting than arriving at the destination.**

BILL HYBELS

---

## THE HEART OF JESUS PRAYS:

*Father, be with this child of Yours who sincerely wants to follow wherever You may lead. Help this one remember that faith is not a road map that You provide ahead of time, but that it's a step-by-step journey. Give this one the grace, understanding, and faith to understand the importance of each step, be it on easy terrain or over a rocky path.*

# 40

---

# I DON'T FEEL
# VERY HAPPY

---

*Everyone focuses on pursuing
"whatever makes you happy." But what does it
mean for a Christian to be happy?*

## THE HEART OF JESUS ANSWERS:

*Those who are pure in their thinking are happy, because they will be with God.*

MATTHEW 5:8 NCV

JESUS

---

Happiness depends less upon our circumstances than upon our thoughts. When we turn our thoughts to God, to His gifts, and to His glorious creation, we experience the joy God intends for His children. But when we focus on the negative aspects of life, we inadvertently bring needless pain to our friends, to our families, and to ourselves.

Do you sincerely want to be a happy person? Then set your mind and your heart upon God's love and His grace. Seek a genuine, intimate, life-altering relationship with your Heavenly Father by studying His Word and trusting His promises. And while you're at it, count your blessings instead of your hardships. Then, after you've done these things, claim the joy, the peace, and the spiritual abundance that the Shepherd offers His sheep.

Jesus came so that you might have an abundant life. Follow Him and seek God's will. When you do these things, your joys will be multiplied.

---

**We will never be happy until we make God
the source of our fulfillment and
the answer to our longings.**

STORMIE OMARTIAN

---

## THE HEART OF JESUS PRAYS:

*Father teach this beloved child that You are not a stern God, but that You are the Creator of joy. You are the Father who wants His child not only to have a happy-ever-after in heaven, but also to enjoy life on earth. May Your Spirit let this child know that You love this one devotedly—and may that knowledge bring happiness and assurance to this child You cherish.*

# 41

HEALTH

# YOU, YOUR BODY,
AND GOD

*If a Christian's focus should be on heaven,
do I really need to worry about how healthy
I am here on earth?*

## THE HEART OF JESUS ANSWERS:

*The thief's purpose is to steal and kill and destroy. My purpose is to give life in all its fullness.*

JOHN 10:10 NLT

JESUS

I n the Book of Romans, Paul encourages us to make our bodies "holy and pleasing to God." Paul adds that to do so is a "spiritual act of worship." This gives believers a clear implication: God intends that we take special care of the bodies He has given us. But it's tempting to do otherwise. We live in a fast-food world where unhealthy choices are convenient, inexpensive, and tempting.

As adults, each of us bears a personal responsibility for the general state of our own physical health. Certainly, various aspects of health are beyond our control: illness sometimes strikes even the healthiest men and women. But for most of us, physical health is a choice: it is the result of hundreds of small decisions that we make every day of our lives. If we make decisions that promote good health, our bodies respond.

Do you sincerely desire to improve your health? If so, start by taking personal responsibility for the body

God has given you. Then pledge to yourself that you will begin to make the changes that are required to enjoy a longer, healthier, happier life. No one can make those changes for you; you must make them for yourself. And with God's help, you can . . . and you will.

Treat your body as God's gift because that's precisely what it is.

---

**If you desire to improve your physical well-being
and your emotional outlook,
increasing your faith can help you.**

JOHN MAXWELL

---

## THE HEART OF JESUS PRAYS:

*Father, the human body, mind, and spirit are so intertwined. Help Your dear one to realize that when a human's body is not at its best shape, the mind, emotions, and even spirit suffer. Help this one know that the best spiritual and personal life on earth often goes hand-in-hand with a healthy body.*

# 42

---

# WHAT IS
# HEAVEN LIKE?

---

*What will heaven be like?*

## THE HEART OF JESUS ANSWERS:

*In My Father's house are many dwelling places; if not, I would have told you. I am going away to prepare a place for you. If I go away and prepare a place for you, I will come back and receive you to Myself, so that where I am you may be also.*

JOHN 14:2-3 HCSB

JESUS

---

S ometimes life's inevitable troubles and heartbreaks are easier to tolerate when we remind ourselves that heaven is our true home. An old hymn contains the words, "This world is not my home; I'm just passing through." Thank goodness!

For believers, death is not an ending; it is a beginning. For believers, the grave is not a final resting-place; it is a place of transition. Death can never claim those who have accepted Christ as their personal Savior. Christ has promised that He has gone to prepare a glorious abode in heaven—a timeless, blessed gift to His children—and Jesus always keeps His promises.

If you've committed your life to Christ, your time here on earth is merely a preparation for a far different life to come: your eternal life with Jesus.

So while this world can be a place of temporary hardship and temporary suffering, you can find comfort in the knowledge that God offers you a permanent home free from all suffering and pain. Please take God at His word. When you do, you can withstand any problem, knowing that your troubles are temporary, but heaven is not.

Even life's happiest experiences last but a moment, yet Heaven's joy is eternal.
Some day we will go to our eternal Home, and Christ will be there to welcome us!

BILLY GRAHAM

## THE HEART OF JESUS PRAYS:

*Father, just as this one finds faith in You for the goodness of life on this earth, may Your Spirit move to build faith in Your heavenly home. May this one truly believe Your Word in 1 Corinthians 2:19, which tells Your children that eyes have not seen, and ears have not heard, and their minds cannot conceive the wonderful things You have been waiting for them when they're in Your presence. Help this fact become a reality in this one's life.*

# 43

# SOWING THE SEEDS OF GENEROSITY

—⚜—

*I see so many people around me who have needs.*
*What should I do?*

## THE HEART OF JESUS ANSWERS:

*The man with two tunics should share with him who has none, and the one who has food should do the same.*

LUKE 3:11 NIV

JESUS

Sometimes we would like to help make the world a better place, but we're not sure of the best way to do it. Jesus told the story of the "Good Samaritan," a man who helped a fellow traveler when no one else would. We, too, should be good Samaritans when we encounter people who need our help.

The words of Jesus are unambiguous: "Freely you have received, freely give" (Matthew 10:8 NIV). As followers of Christ, we are commanded to be generous with our friends, with our families, and with those in need. We must give freely of our time, our possessions, and, most especially, our love.

In 2 Corinthians 9:6-7, Paul reminds us that when we sow the seeds of generosity, we reap bountiful rewards in accordance with God's plan for our lives: "Now this I say, he who sows sparingly will also reap sparingly, and he who sows bountifully will also reap bountifully. Each one must do just as he has purposed in his heart, not grudgingly or under compulsion, for God loves a cheerful giver" (KJV).

Today, take God's words to heart and make this pledge: Wherever you happen to be, be a good Samaritan. Somebody near you needs your assistance, and you need the spiritual rewards that will be yours when you lend a helping hand.

---

**Do all the good you can. By all the means you can.**
**In all the ways you can. In all the places you can.**
**At all the times you can. To all the people you can.**
**As long as ever you can.**

JOHN WESLEY

---

## THE HEART OF JESUS PRAYS:

*Father, it is so easy for Your dear ones on earth to want to help others…but to become too busy, or to assume that someone else will shoulder the burden, or to feel that their help wouldn't be enough, so they might as well not try at all. Help this one see needs and seek Your guidance on meeting those needs. Remind Your children that as they help others, they are being Your hands and feet.*

# 44

---

# SHOWING PROPER
# RESPECT TO GOD

*What does it mean to honor God?*

## THE HEART OF JESUS ANSWERS:

*The one who loves his life will lose it, and the one who hates his life in this world will keep it for eternal life. If anyone serves Me, he must follow Me. Where I am, there My servant also will be. If anyone serves Me, the Father will honor him.*

JOHN 12:25-26 HCSB

JESUS

———— ❦ ————

At times, your life is probably hectic, demanding, and complicated. When the demands of life leave you rushing from place to place with scarcely a moment to spare, you may fail to pause and thank your Creator for the blessings He has bestowed upon you. But that's a big mistake.

Who will you choose to honor today? If you honor God and place Him at the center of your life, every day is a cause for celebration. But if you fail to honor your Heavenly Father, you're asking for trouble, and lots of it. So honor God for who He is and for what He has done for you. And don't just honor Him on Sunday morning. Praise Him all day long, every day, for as long as you live . . . and then for all eternity.

Today and every day, give your Father in heaven the honor He deserves. When you do, you will be blessed now and forever.

---

**Praise opens the window of our hearts,
preparing us to walk more closely with God.
Prayer raises the window of our spirit,
enabling us to listen more clearly to the Father.**

MAX LUCADO

---

## THE HEART OF JESUS PRAYS:

*Father, Your children on earth like to be appreciated and often forget that You know what that's like. Help this one You love develop the attitude of gratitude. Open this one's eyes to the wonderful things You do, and may Your Spirit prompt Your child to acknowledge that all good gifts come from You.*

# 45

JESUS

# WHAT A FRIEND

*Jesus, what should I know about You?*

## THE HEART OF JESUS ANSWERS:

*If anyone desires to come after Me, let him deny himself, and take up his cross daily, and follow Me. For whoever desires to save his life will lose it, but whoever loses his life for My sake will save it.*

LUKE 9:23-24 NKJV

JESUS

---

The 19th-century writer Hannah Whitall Smith observed, "The crucial question for each of us is this: What do you think of Jesus, and do you yet have a personal acquaintance with Him?" Indeed, the answer to that question determines the quality, the course, and the direction of our lives today and for all eternity.

The old familiar hymn begins, "What a friend we have in Jesus...." No truer words were ever penned. Jesus is the sovereign Friend and ultimate Savior of mankind. Christ showed enduring love for His believers by willingly sacrificing His own life so that we might have eternal life. Now, it is our turn to become His friend.

Let us love our Savior, praise Him, and share His message of salvation with our neighbors and with the world. When we do, we demonstrate that our acquaintance with the Master is not a passing fancy; it is, instead, the cornerstone and the touchstone of our lives.

Jesus Christ loves you. He is your comforter and your best friend. He wants you to spend eternity with Him in heaven. Follow Him.

———⟨⟩———

**Jesus: the proof of God's love.**

PHILIP YANCEY

———⟨⟩———

## THE HEART OF JESUS PRAYS:

*Father, friendship is such a precious relationship. It warms the heart and gives Your people on earth a sense of being part of a group—which in turns gives them strength to handle life's challenges. Open this one's eyes to realize that You are the best friend that they have, and that I am present at all times.*

# 46

JOY

# WHY DON'T I FEEL JOYFUL?

*The world is a scary place.*
*Why should I be joyful?*

## THE HEART OF JESUS ANSWERS:

*These things I have spoken to you, that My joy may remain in you, and that your joy may be full.*

JOHN 15:11 NKJV

JESUS

---

Have you made the choice to rejoice? Hopefully so. After all, if you're a believer, you have plenty of reasons to be joyful. Yet sometimes, amid the inevitable hustle and bustle of life here on earth, you may lose sight of your blessings as you wrestle with the challenges of everyday life.

Christ made it clear to His followers: He intended that His joy would become their joy. And it still holds true today: Christ intends that His believers share His love with His joy in their hearts.

What does life have in store for you? A world full of possibilities (of course it's up to you to seize them), and God's promise of abundance (of course it's up to you to accept it). So, as you embark upon the next phase of your journey, remember to celebrate the life that God has given you. Your Creator has blessed you beyond measure. Honor Him with your prayers, your words, your deeds, and your joy.

Joy does not depend upon your circumstances, but upon your relationship with God. When you love the Lord and follow Jesus, you'll experience a joyful peace that can be found in no other way.

---

**A life of intimacy with God
is characterized by joy.**

OSWALD CHAMBERS

---

## THE HEART OF JESUS PRAYS:

*Father, the enemy wants this dear one to believe that the world is bad and life is bad...and that the future will be bad. May Your Spirit prompt this one to realize that though sin and evil may be obvious in the world, Your grace and power still reign. You are mightily at work, and You will triumph over the enemy. Please make this a reality in this child's life so that he or she can rejoice and confidently serve you.*

# 47

## JUDGING OTHERS

# I AM TOO JUDGMENTAL

*It's hard not to judge people and their motives.
Is it always wrong to judge others?*

## THE HEART OF JESUS ANSWERS:

*Do not judge, or you too will be judged. For in the same way you judge others, you will be judged, and with the measure you use, it will be measured to you.*

The warning of Matthew 7:1 is clear: "Judge not, that ye be not judged" (KJV). Yet even the most devoted Christians may fall prey to a powerful yet subtle temptation: the temptation to judge others. But as obedient followers of Christ, we are commanded to refrain from such behavior.

As Jesus came upon a young woman who had been condemned by the Pharisees, He spoke not only to the crowd that was gathered there, but also to all generations when He warned, "He that is without sin among you, let him first cast a stone at her" (John 8:7 KJV). Christ's message is clear, and it applies not only to the Pharisees of ancient times, but also to us.

Your ability to judge others requires a divine insight that you simply don't have. So do everybody (including yourself) a favor: don't judge.

# Christians think they are prosecuting attorneys or judges, when, in reality, God has called all of us to be witnesses.

WARREN WIERSBE

---

## THE HEART OF JESUS PRAYS:

*Father, when Your child feels prone to condemn others for the way they behave or seem to be, may Your Spirit send a reminder that You are still working in human hearts and that appearances can be deceptive. When Your child sees fruit indicating that people may not be in right standing with You, help Your child develop the habit of praying for them.*

# 48

---

LISTENING TO GOD

# HOW DO I HEAR GOD?

---

*What do I need to know about*
*listening to God and following Jesus?*

## THE HEART OF JESUS ANSWERS:

*Take my yoke upon you and learn from me…*

MATTHEW 11:29 NIV

JESUS

---

Sometimes, God displays His wishes in ways that are undeniable. But on other occasions, God's hand is much more subtle. Sometimes, God speaks to us in quiet tones, and when He does, we are well advised to listen . . . carefully.

Do you take time each day for an extended period of silence? And during those precious moments, do you sincerely open your heart to your Creator? If so, you are wise and you are blessed.

The world can be a noisy place, a place filled to the brim with distractions, interruptions, and frustrations. And if you're not careful, the struggles and stresses of everyday living can rob you of the peace that should rightfully be yours because of your personal relationship with Christ. So take time each day to quietly commune with your Savior. When you do, you will most certainly encounter the subtle hand of God, and if you are wise, you will let His hand lead you along the path that He has chosen.

When you're communicating with God, try to listen more and talk less.

---

**When we come to Jesus stripped of pretensions,**
**with a needy spirit, ready to listen,**
**He meets us at the point of need.**

CATHERINE MARSHALL

---

## THE HEART OF JESUS PRAYS:

*Father, help Your child learn to recognize Your voice and to discern Your voice through all the clamoring noise of life. Give Your child a sense of the realness of relationship with You . . . to know that when he or she prays, You hear and answer, and to recognize the ways You are speaking directly to him or her. May Your Spirit grow that intimacy and trust in this one's life.*

# 49

---

LOVE

# I DON'T FEEL
# VERY LOVING

---

*I've heard the Bible tells us to love others.*
*Is it really that important?*

## THE HEART OF JESUS ANSWERS:

*A new commandment I give unto you, that ye love one another; as I have loved you, that ye also love one another.*

JOHN 13:34 KJV

JESUS

---

Love, like everything else in this wonderful world, begins and ends with God, but the middle part belongs to us. During the brief time that we have here on earth, God has given each of us the opportunity to become a loving person—or not. God has given each of us the opportunity to be kind, to be courteous, to be cooperative, and to be forgiving—or not.

God has given each of us the chance to obey the Golden Rule, or to make up our own rules as we go. If we obey God's rules, we're safe, but if we do otherwise, we're headed for trouble and fast.

Here in the real world, the choices that we make have consequences. The decisions that we make and the results of those decisions determine the quality of our relationships. It's as simple as that.

God is love, and He expects you to share His love with others. He wants you to love your neighbors without conditions or reservation. And when you do, the Lord will bless you and keep you, now and forever.

---

**Love is an attribute of God.**
**To love others is evidence of a genuine faith.**

KAY ARTHUR

---

## THE HEART OF JESUS PRAYS:

*Father, love is not always easy for Your ones who live on earth, but it is always worth the struggles and sacrifices it may cause. Help Your child realize that love is not just a feeling but a commitment to others and service to them. And may Your child feel the overwhelming sense of love from You and others.*

# 50

# WHAT DO YOU GIVE THE GOD WHO HAS EVERYTHING?

*How can you have a relationship with the One who is the most powerful Being through all of time? That's hard to wrap my head around!*

## THE HEART OF JESUS ANSWERS:

*You shall love the Lord your God with all your heart, with all your soul, and with all your mind. This is the greatest and most important commandment.*

MATTHEW 22:37-38 HCSB

JESUS

———

C. S. Lewis observed, "A person's spiritual health is exactly proportional to his love for God." If we are to enjoy the spiritual health that God intends for us, we should keep Lewis' words in mind.

Corrie ten Boom noted, "A bird does not know it can fly before it uses its wings. We learn God's love in our hearts as soon as we act upon it." She understood that whenever we worship God with our hearts and our minds, we are blessed by our love for Him and His love for us.

Today, open your heart to the Father. And let your obedience be a fitting response to His never-ending love. And, while you're at it, tell the world how you have been touched and transformed by the incredible sacrifice of His Son.

God loves you, and He wants you to love Him back. If you sincerely love the Lord, don't be afraid to tell Him so.

---

**What is Christian perfection?
Loving God with all our heart,
mind, soul, and strength.**

JOHN WESLEY

---

## THE HEART OF JESUS PRAYS:

*Father, humans know at heart that they're prone to sin and make errors. And the enemy taunts them about that. So it's very hard for them to believe that You and I really love them—just as they are. Today may Your Spirit give this precious one such a sense of Your extreme love. May Your Spirit prompt in his or her heart the realization that We love this one so much I would have died on the cross if this one had been the only sinner on earth.*

# 51

MATERIALISM

# I SPEND MONEY ON THINGS I REALLY DON'T NEED

*We live in a materialistic world.*
*How can I escape the traps of materialism?*

## THE HEART OF JESUS ANSWERS:

*Watch out and be on guard against all greed, because one's life is not in the abundance of his possessions.*

LUKE 12:15 HCSB

JESUS

How important are your material possessions? Not as important as you might think. In the life of a committed Christian, material possessions should play a rather small role. In fact, when we become overly enamored with the things we own, we needlessly distance ourselves from the peace God offers to those who place Him at the center of their lives.

Of course, we all need the basic necessities of life, but once we meet those needs for ourselves and for our families, the piling up of possessions creates more problems than it solves. Our real riches, of course, are not of this world. We are never really rich until we are rich in spirit.

Do you find yourself wrapped up in the concerns of the material world? If so, it's time to reorder your priorities by turning your thoughts and your prayers to more important matters. And, it's time to begin storing up riches that will endure throughout eternity: the spiritual kind.

Material possessions may seem appealing as we gain them, but they pale in comparison to the spiritual gifts that God gives to those who put Him first.

⎯⎯⎯⎯ ⎯⎯⎯⎯

> **If you want to be truly happy, you won't find it**
> **on an endless quest for more stuff.**
> **You'll find it in receiving God's generosity**
> **and in passing that generosity along.**
>
> BILL HYBELS

⎯⎯⎯⎯ ⎯⎯⎯⎯

## THE HEART OF JESUS PRAYS:

*Father, it's so hard for Your dear ones on earth to find the balance between using possessions for good . . . and practically worshipping them as a status of success. May Your Spirit whisper to Your dear one's heart the truth that treasures are to be used for Your glory—not sought ahead of You.*

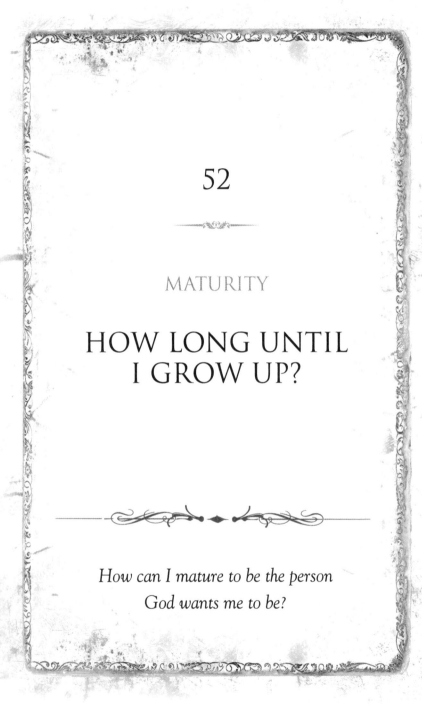

52

MATURITY

# HOW LONG UNTIL
# I GROW UP?

*How can I mature to be the person
God wants me to be?*

## THE HEART OF JESUS ANSWERS:

*If you cling to your life, you will lose it; but if you give it up for me, you will find it.*

MATTHEW 10:39 NLT

JESUS

―――――――――✦―――――――――

The journey toward spiritual maturity is a long one. In fact, it lasts a lifetime. As Christians we can—and should—continue to grow in the love and the knowledge of our Savior as long as we live. Norman Vincent Peale had this advice for believers of all ages: "Ask the God who made you to keep remaking you." That advice, of course, is perfectly sound, but often ignored.

When we cease to grow, either emotionally or spiritually, we do ourselves a profound disservice. But, if we study God's Word, if we obey His commandments, and if we live in the center of His will, we will not be "stagnant" believers; we will, instead, be growing Christians . . . and that's exactly what God intends for us to be.

Life is a series of choices and decisions. Each day, we make countless decisions that can bring us closer to God . . . or not. When we live according to the principles contained in God's Holy Word, we embark upon a journey of spiritual maturity that results in life abundant and life eternal.

God is still working in you and through you. Even if you're a mature Christian, you can still grow in the knowledge and love of your Lord.

---

**God's plan for our guidance is
for us to grow gradually in wisdom
before we get to the crossroads.**

BILL HYBELS

---

## THE HEART OF JESUS PRAYS:

*Father, the longer Your dear one knows You, the more this one resembles You. May Your Spirit teach this one that ups and downs are part of the process of becoming more like You, and becoming closer to You.*

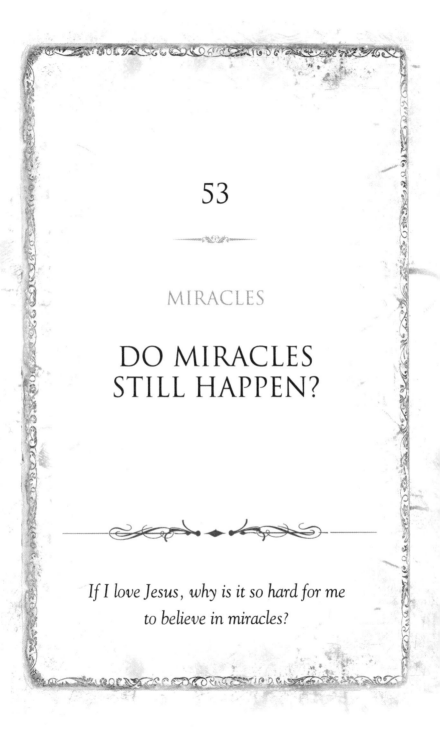

53

MIRACLES

# DO MIRACLES STILL HAPPEN?

*If I love Jesus, why is it so hard for me to believe in miracles?*

## THE HEART OF JESUS ANSWERS:

*With men it is impossible, but not with God, because all things are possible with God.*

MARK 10:27 HCSB

JESUS

I f you haven't seen any of God's miracles lately, you haven't been looking. Throughout history the Creator has intervened in the course of human events in ways that cannot be explained by science or human rationale. And He's still doing so today.

God's miracles are not limited to special occasions, nor are they witnessed by a select few. God is crafting His wonders all around us: the miracle of the birth of a new baby; the miracle of a world renewing itself with every sunrise; the miracle of lives transformed by God's love and grace. Each day, God's handiwork is evident for all to see and experience.

Today, seize the opportunity to inspect God's hand at work. His miracles come in a variety of shapes and sizes, so keep your eyes and your heart open. Be watchful, and you'll soon be amazed.

Nothing is too hard for God. If you're looking for miracles, you'll find them. If you're not, you won't.

When God is involved,
anything can happen.
Be open and stay that way.
God has a beautiful way of
bringing good vibrations
out of broken chords.

—

CHARLES SWINDOLL

**THE HEART OF JESUS PRAYS:**

*Father, help this one realize that not only do You perform miracles, but You perform miracles through Your children all the time—through their prayer and actions. May You give this child a sense of not only believing in and recognizing miracles, but being part of the miracles!*

# 54

---

# SHARE YOUR FAITH

*I don't get what the big deal is about missions.*
*Why are people always talking about this?*

## THE HEART OF JESUS ANSWERS:

*All authority in heaven and on earth has been given to me. Therefore go and make disciples of all nations, baptizing them in the name of the Father and of the Son and of the Holy Spirit, and teaching them to obey everything I have commanded you. And surely I am with you always, to the very end of the age.*

MATTHEW 28:18-20 NIV

JESUS

———————

The Good News of Jesus Christ should be shouted from the rooftops by believers the world over. But all too often, it is not. For a variety of reasons, many Christians keep their beliefs to themselves, and when they do, the world suffers because of their failure to speak up.

As believers, we are called to share the transforming message of Jesus with our families, with our neighbors, and with the world. Jesus commands us to become fishers of men. And, the time to go fishing is now. We must share the Good News of Jesus Christ today—tomorrow may indeed be too late.

God will empower you to share your faith. This very day, He will provide surprising opportunities to tell the world about His love and His Son. When those opportunities arise, and they will, be bold. The time for missions is now.

<hr>

Our commission is quite specific.
We are told to be His witness to all nations.
For us, as His disciples, to refuse any part of
this commission frustrates the love of
Jesus Christ, the Son of God.

CATHERINE MARSHALL

<hr>

## THE HEART OF JESUS PRAYS:

*Father, help Your child realize that missionaries aren't just sent, they're born—born again, that is! All people who claim Your name are missionaries in their own way. Open this dear one's eyes to the opportunities in everyday life to let others know about You.*

# 55

MISTAKES

# I BLEW IT AGAIN!

*I've made mistakes. What should I do?*

## THE HEART OF JESUS ANSWERS:

*I assure you, unless you turn from your sins and become as little children, you will never get into the Kingdom of Heaven.*

MATTHEW 18:2-3 NLT

JESUS

Everybody makes mistakes, and so will you. In fact, Winston Churchill once observed, "Success is going from failure to failure without loss of enthusiasm." You should expect to make mistakes—plenty of mistakes—but you should not let those missteps rob you of the enthusiasm you need to fulfill God's plan for your life.

We are imperfect people living in an imperfect world; mistakes are simply part of the price we pay for being here. But, even though mistakes are an inevitable part of life's journey, repeated mistakes should not be. When we commit the inevitable blunders of life, we must correct them, learn from them, and pray for the wisdom not to repeat them. When we do, our mistakes become lessons, and our lives become adventures in growth, not stagnation.

Have you made a mistake or three? Of course you have. But here's the big question: have you used your mistakes as stumbling blocks or stepping stones? The answer to that question will determine how well you will perform in the workplace and in every other aspect of your life.

If you've broken one of God's rules, you can always ask Him for His forgiveness. And He will always give it!

---

**God is able to take mistakes, when they are committed to Him, and make of them something for our good and for His glory.**

RUTH BELL GRAHAM

---

## THE HEART OF JESUS PRAYS:

*Father, the enemy torments Your children when they make mistakes and have other failures. Sometimes the enemy's voice is so strong. But help Your child to listen beyond the enemy's taunts to hear Your voice and learn from the errors. May Your Spirit show Your dear one how to get up and keep going, striving toward the goals You have planned.*

# 56

## OBEDIENCE

# OBEDIENCE NOW

*Sometimes it's hard to be obey.*
*How can I be a more obedient Christian?*

## THE HEART OF JESUS ANSWERS:

*Anyone who listens to my teaching and obeys me is wise, like a person who builds a house on solid rock. Though the rain comes in torrents and the floodwaters rise and the winds beat against that house, it won't collapse, because it is built on rock.*

MATTHEW 7:24-25 NLT

JESUS

---

We live in a noisy, troubled world. In our world peace can be a scarce commodity—but it doesn't have to be that way. The Bible promises that we can find peace when we trust God's promises and obey His commandments. But the Bible also issues a warning: If we don't pay much attention to God's Word, or if we rebel against His teachings, we may forfeit countless blessings that would have otherwise been ours.

Would you like to enjoy the genuine, lasting peace that only God can provide? Then study His Word and honor Him with your actions. When you do, you'll soon discover that obedience is the path to peace. It always has been, and it always will be.

God rewards obedience and punishes disobedience. It's not enough to understand God's rules; you must also live by them.

———

**Trials and sufferings teach us to obey the Lord by faith, and we soon learn that obedience pays off in joyful ways.**

BILL BRIGHT

———

## THE HEART OF JESUS PRAYS:

*Father, obedience has been hard for humans since Eve first questioned Your commands in the Garden of Eden. Be with this dear child of Yours. May Your Spirit help this one see beyond the lure of the enemy. May Your Spirit empower his beloved child to seek You, to turn to You, and to obey You, even in the midst of temptation.*

# 57

# I FEEL OVERWHELMED BY NEGATIVE THOUGHTS

*Why do so many Christians seem
so optimistic about everything?*

## THE HEART OF JESUS ANSWERS:

*These things I have spoken to you, that in Me you may have peace. In the world you will have tribulation; but be of good cheer, I have overcome the world.*

JOHN 16:33 NKJV

JESUS

**P**essimism and Christianity don't mix. Why? Because Christians have every reason to be optimistic about life here on earth and life eternal. Lettie Cowman (who wrote under the name of Mrs. Charles E. Cowman) advised, "Never yield to gloomy anticipation. Place your hope and confidence in God. He has no record of failure."

Sometimes, despite our trust in God, we may fall into the spiritual traps of worry, frustration, anxiety, or sheer exhaustion, and our hearts become heavy. At those times we need plenty of rest, a large dose of perspective, and God's healing touch—but not necessarily in that order.

Today, make this promise to yourself and keep it: vow to be a hope-filled Christian. Think optimistically about your life, your education, your family, and your future. Trust your hopes, not your fears. Take time to celebrate God's glorious creation. And then, when you've filled your heart with hope, share your optimism with others. They'll be better for it, and so will you.

You will encounter occasional disappointments, and, from time to time, you will encounter failure. But, don't invest large quantities of your life focusing on past misfortunes. Instead, look to the future with optimism and hope.

*The people whom I have seen succeed best in life have always been cheerful and hopeful people who went about their business with a smile on their faces.*

CHARLES KINGSLEY

## THE HEART OF JESUS PRAYS:

*Father, when Your beloved child has the option of choosing between the negative and positive perspectives of life or a situation, help this one remember that You are the ultimately powerful Being and that nothing is impossible for You. Therefore, Your children can rejoice and be optimistic, knowing that with Us at their side, nothing is impossible, and life is full of hope.*

# 58

# WHY DO I CARE WHAT OTHERS THINK?

*Peer pressure seems to be everywhere,
and it's usually negative.
How can I move beyond it?*

## THE HEART OF JESUS ANSWERS:

*You make yourselves look good in front of people, but God knows what is really in your hearts. What is important to people is hateful in God's sight.*

LUKE 16:15 NCV

JESUS

Our world is filled with pressures: some good, some bad. The pressures that we feel to follow God's will and to behave responsibly are positive pressures. God places them on our hearts, and He intends that we act accordingly. But we also face different pressures, ones that are definitely not from God. When we feel pressured to do things—or even to think thoughts—that lead us away from God, we must beware.

Society seeks to mold us into the cookie-cutter images that are the product of the modern media. God seeks to mold us into new beings, new creations through Christ, beings that are most certainly not conformed to this world. If we want to please God, we must resist the pressures that society seeks to impose upon us. Instead, we need to conform ourselves, instead, to His will, to His path, and to His Son.

Your world is filled with pressures, some good and some bad. When you follow Jesus, you will learn the difference between good peer pressure and bad peer pressure . . . and you'll learn to act accordingly.

---

**Those who follow the crowd usually get lost in it.**

RICK WARREN

---

## THE HEART OF JESUS PRAYS:

*Father, earthly struggles allow Your children to learn of Your strength and Your power. And, adversity teaches them what Your power really means in their own lives. May Your Spirit help them rely on You so they can confidently overcome hardship and live godly lives in all circumstances.*

# 59

PERSEVERANCE

# HOW DO I KEEP GOING WHEN I FEEL LIKE QUITTING?

*Sometimes I'm tempted to give up.*
*How can I hang in there?*

## THE HEART OF JESUS ANSWERS:

*Don't look for shortcuts to God. The market is flooded with surefire, easygoing formulas for a successful life that can be practiced in your spare time. Don't fall for that stuff, even though crowds of people do. The way to life—to God!—is vigorous and requires total attention.*

MATTHEW 7:13-14 MSG

JESUS

Are you one of those people who doesn't give up easily, or are you quick to bail out when the going gets tough? If you've developed the unfortunate habit of giving up at the first sign of trouble, it's probably time for you to have a heart-to-heart talk with the guy (or gal) you see every time you look in the mirror.

A well-lived life is like a marathon, not a sprint—it calls for preparation, determination, and lots of diligence. As an example of perfect perseverance, you need look no further than your Savior, Jesus Christ.

Jesus finished what He began, and so should you. Christ was unwavering in His faithfulness to God. You, too, should remain faithful, especially when times are tough.

Are you facing a difficult situation? If so, remember this: whatever your problem, God can handle it. Your job is to keep persevering until He does.

If things don't work out at first, don't quit. If you don't keep trying, you'll never know what you and Jesus, working together, could have accomplished.

---

Perseverance is more than endurance.
It is endurance combined with absolute assurance
and certainty that what we are looking
for is going to happen.

OSWALD CHAMBERS

---

## THE HEART OF JESUS PRAYS:

*Father, as this dear one hangs on to Your words, Your will, and Your service, may Your Spirit give him or her the sense that he or she is not hanging alone...that You're right there holding Your child up until the tough stuff is over.*

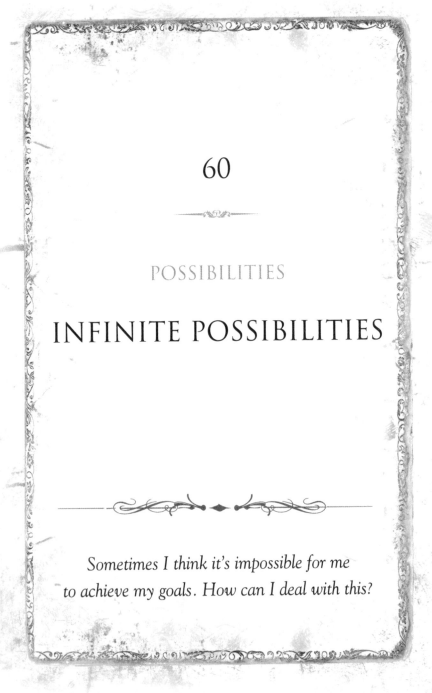

# 60

POSSIBILITIES

# INFINITE POSSIBILITIES

*Sometimes I think it's impossible for me
to achieve my goals. How can I deal with this?*

## THE HEART OF JESUS ANSWERS:

*If you have faith as a mustard seed, you will say to this mountain, "Move from here to there," and it will move; and nothing will be impossible for you.*

MATTHEW 17:20 NKJV

JESUS

A re you afraid to ask God to do big things in your life? Is your faith threadbare and worn? If so, it's time to abandon your doubts and reclaim your faith in God's promises.

Ours is a God of infinite possibilities. But sometimes, because of limited faith and limited understanding, we wrongly assume that God cannot or will not intervene in the affairs of mankind. Those assumptions are simply wrong.

God's Holy Word makes it clear: absolutely nothing is impossible for the Lord. And since the Bible means what it says, you can be comforted in the knowledge that the Creator of the universe can do miraculous things in your own life and in the lives of your loved ones. Your challenge, as a believer, is to take God at His word, and to expect the miraculous.

Nothing is impossible for God, so don't be afraid to dream big dreams, and don't be afraid to pray for a miracle. After all, prayer can move mountains. And, the possibilities that surround you are limitless.

———

**God's faithfulness and grace make
the impossible possible.**

SHEILA WALSH

———

## THE HEART OF JESUS PRAYS:

*Father, remind this dear one that, just as You are the God of the impossible, this beloved one is the child of the God of the impossible. And as Your child, this one has spiritually inherited the gift of seeing unbelievable things happen. Help Your children believe in miracles...even in their own lives!*

# 61

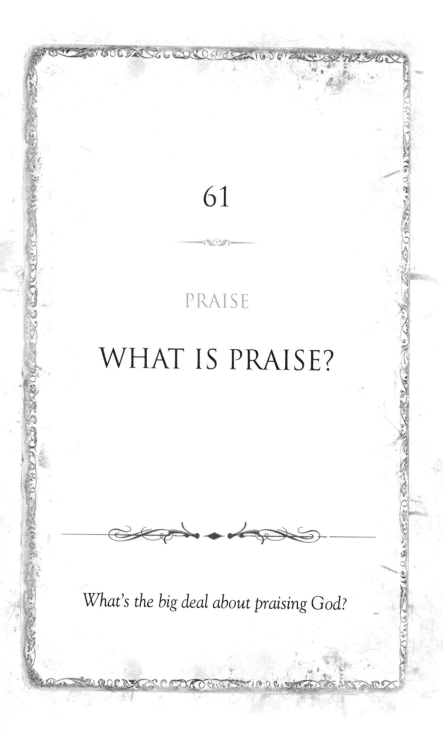

## PRAISE

# WHAT IS PRAISE?

*What's the big deal about praising God?*

## THE HEART OF JESUS ANSWERS:

*You shall love the Lord your God with all your heart, with all your soul, and with all your mind. This is the greatest and most important commandment.*

MATTHEW 22:37-38 HCSB

JESUS

B ecause we have been saved by God's only Son, we must never lose hope in the priceless gifts of eternal love and eternal life. And, because we are so richly blessed, we must approach our Heavenly Father with reverence and thanksgiving.

Sometimes, in our rush "to get things done," we simply don't stop long enough to pause and thank our Creator for the countless blessings He has bestowed upon us. But when we slow down and express our gratitude to the One who made us, we enrich our own lives and the lives of those around us.

Thanksgiving should become a habit, a regular part of our daily routines. God has blessed us beyond measure, and we owe Him everything, including our eternal praise. Let us praise Him today, tomorrow, and throughout eternity.

God deserves your praise . . . and you deserve the experience of praising Him.

⸺⸙⸺

**The time for universal praise is
sure to come some day.
Let us begin to do our part now.**
HANNAH WHITALL SMITH

⸺⸙⸺

## THE HEART OF JESUS PRAYS:

*Father, help Your child realize that saying those magic words "thank You" is not something You require to feed some ego need. Instead, may Your Spirit show Your beloved one that when people form the habit of thanking You, they start seeing Your presence more and more. May this one learn that acknowledging Your goodness makes faith grow!*

# 62

PRAYER

# THE QUESTIONS
# GOD LOVES TO ANSWER

*Can prayer really change my life?*

## THE HEART OF JESUS ANSWERS:

*And everything—whatever you ask in prayer, believing—you will receive.*

MATTHEW 21:22 HCSB

JESUS

---

This fast-paced, troubled world desperately needs your prayers, and so does your family. When you weave the habit of prayer into the very fabric of your day, you invite God to become a partner in every aspect of your life. When you consult God on an constant basis, you avail yourself of His wonderful wisdom, His strength, and His love. And, because God answers prayers according to His perfect timetable, your petitions to your Heavenly Father will transform your family, your friends, your world, and yourself.

Today, turn everything over to your Heavenly Father in prayer. Instead of worrying about your next decision, decide to let God lead the way. Don't limit your prayers to meals or to bedtime. Pray constantly about things great and small. God is listening, and He wants to hear from you. Now.

Prayer changes things and it will change you. So pray. So pray often, pray early, keep the faith, and trust in God. When you do these things, you won't be disappointed.

———◦◦◦———

**Two wings are necessary to lift our souls toward God: prayer and praise. Prayer asks. Praise accepts the answer.**

MRS. CHARLES E. COWMAN

———◦◦◦———

## THE HEART OF JESUS PRAYS:

*Father, sometimes humans think that something has to be complicated to be good; that they have to make great, difficult sacrifices to achieve results. May Your Spirit teach this one that those short, simple, fleeting prayers during the day affect the life—and eternity—of the one praying and those prayed for.*

# 63

PRIORITIES

# WHO'S ON FIRST?

*How can I set my priorities in the right way…*
*and keep them strong?*

## THE HEART OF JESUS ANSWERS:

*Love the Lord your God with all your heart, all your soul, and all your mind. This is the first and most important command. And the second command is like the first: Love your neighbor as you love yourself. All the law and the writings of the prophets depend on these two commands.*

MATTHEW 22:37-40 NCV

JESUS

<hr/>

J esus made a sacrifice for you. Are you willing to make sacrifices for Him? Can you honestly say that you're passionate about your faith and that you're really following Jesus? Hopefully so. But if you're preoccupied with other things—or if you're strictly a one-day-a-week Christian—then it's time to reorder your priorities.

Nothing is more important than your wholehearted commitment to your Creator and to His only begotten Son. Your faith must never be an afterthought; it must be your ultimate priority, your ultimate possession, and your ultimate passion. You are the recipient of Christ's love. Accept it enthusiastically and share it passionately. Jesus deserves your extreme enthusiasm; the world deserves it; and you deserve the experience of sharing it with others.

Your Heavenly Father wants you to prioritize your day and your life. And the best place to start is by putting God first.

---

**It's sobering to contemplate how much time, effort, sacrifice, compromise, and attention we give to acquiring and increasing our supply of something that is totally insignificant in eternity.**

ANNE GRAHAM LOTZ

---

## THE HEART OF JESUS PRAYS:

*Father, help Your beloved learn that sacrifices made to draw closer to You are not really sacrifices. May Your Spirit help this one feel the joy—and resulting benefits—of wholeheartedly pursuing You.*

# 64

---

## PROBLEMS

# PROBLEM-SOLVING 101

---

*Everybody, including me, has problems.*
*How should we handle challenges in our lives?*

## THE HEART OF JESUS ANSWERS:

*Come to me, all you who are weary and burdened, and I will give you rest. Take my yoke upon you and learn from me, for I am gentle and humble in heart, and you will find rest for your souls. For my yoke is easy and my burden is light.*

MATTHEW 11:28-30 NIV

JESUS

Here's a riddle: What is it that is too unimportant to pray about yet too big for God to handle? The answer: nothing. Yet sometimes, when the challenges of the day seem overwhelming, we may spend more time worrying about our troubles than praying about them. And, we may spend more time fretting about our problems than solving them. A far better strategy, of course, is to pray as if everything depended entirely upon God and to work as if everything depended entirely upon us.

When we learn to see our problems as God sees them—as opportunities for transformation and growth—we begin to change our lives and our world. And the best day to begin that transformation is the present one.

Life can be hard, but heaven is forever, so don't let problems get you down. And one more thing: when it comes to solving those problems, work beats worry.

———

**Winners see an answer for every problem; losers see a problem in every answer.**
BARBARA JOHNSON

———

## THE HEART OF JESUS PRAYS:

*Father, sometimes the enemy tempts Your children to think their problems are too little, or too big, for You. In those moments, may Your Spirit remind them that You cared about the tiny birds others thought were insignificant, and how much more You care about Your human creations! Remind them that You were powerful enough to create the universe and keep it running—and You're able to help them handle whatever they face.*

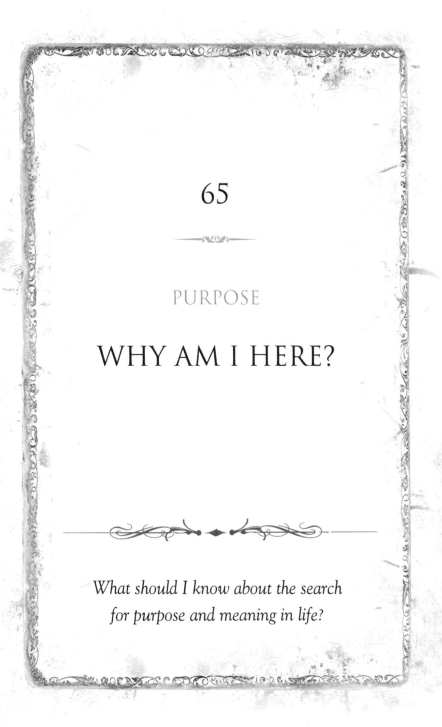

65

PURPOSE

# WHY AM I HERE?

*What should I know about the search*
*for purpose and meaning in life?*

## THE HEART OF JESUS ANSWERS:

*These things have I spoken unto you, that my joy might remain in you, and that your joy might be full.*

JOHN 15:11 KJV

JESUS

"What on earth does God intend for me to do with my life?" This is an easy question to ask, but it can be a difficult question to answer. Why? Because God's purposes aren't always clear to us. Sometimes we wander aimlessly in a wilderness of our own making. And sometimes, we struggle mightily against God in an unsuccessful attempt to find success and happiness through our own means, not His.

Are you genuinely trying to figure out God's purpose for your life? If so, you can be sure that with God's help, you will eventually discover it. So keep praying, and keep watching. And while you're at it, guard your steps by making sure that you're obeying all of God's rules, not just the ones that are easy or convenient. When you do these things, you can rest assured that God will eventually make His plans known to you—and you'll be eternally grateful that He did.

God has a wonderful plan for your life. And, the time to start looking for that plan—and living it—is now.

---

**Continually restate to yourself
what the purpose of your life is.**
OSWALD CHAMBERS

---

## THE HEART OF JESUS PRAYS:

*Father, may Your Spirit help Your dear child not get caught up on knowing all the answers to life right now. May You help this one realize that following Your will is a step-by-step process, and it just might be that Your children may not understand the full purpose of their lives until they look back upon them, while standing in Your presence.*

# 66

━━ ◆ ━━

## PUTTING GOD FIRST

# I FORGET TO PUT
# GOD FIRST

*I have so many things to do, so many people
who depend on me, and feel so overwhelmed.
Any tips on arranging my priorities?*

## THE HEART OF JESUS ANSWERS:

*The thing you should want most is God's kingdom and doing what God wants. Then all these other things you need will be given to you.*

MATTHEW 6:33 NCV

JESUS

Jesus makes it perfectly clear: God should be your first priority.

Have you decided to honor God by giving His Son your heart, your soul, your talents, and your time? Or are you in the habit of giving God little more than a few hours on Sunday mornings? The answers to these questions will determine how you prioritize your time and how you prioritize your life.

Whether you're at work, at home, or someplace in between, you're engaged in worship. In fact, all of mankind is engaged in worship—of one sort or another.

In the book of Exodus, God warns that we should place no gods before Him. Yet all too often, we place our Lord in second, third, or fourth place as we worship the gods of pride, greed, power, or lust. When we place our desires for material possessions above our love for God—or when we yield to the countless temptations that surround us—we find ourselves engaged in a struggle that is similar to the one Jesus faced when He was tempted by Satan. In the wilderness, Satan offered Jesus earthly power and unimaginable riches, but Jesus turned Satan away and chose instead to worship God. We must do likewise by putting God first and worshiping only Him.

---

**The manifold rewards of a serious, consistent prayer life demonstrate clearly that time with our Lord should be our first priority.**

SHIRLEY DOBSON

---

## THE HEART OF JESUS PRAYS:

*Father, when Your child feels overwhelmed with the necessities of life, I ask that You send Your Spirit to calm this one. May this child immediately turn to You for guidance and wisdom for each moment. May Your Spirit guide Your beloved step by step, through all the challenges and needs . . . in the perfect order.*

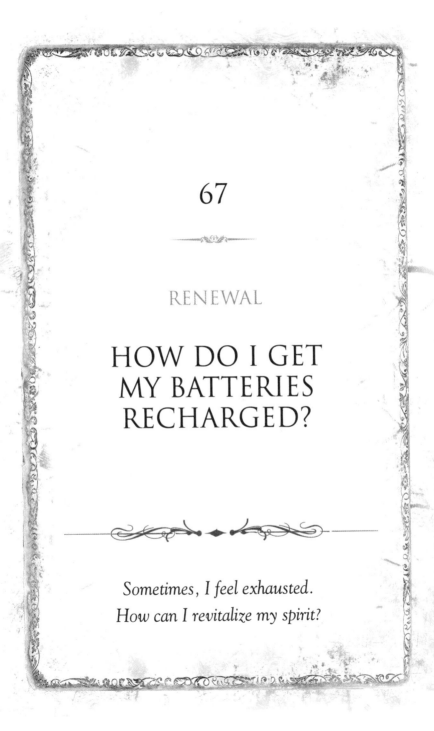

67

RENEWAL

# HOW DO I GET MY BATTERIES RECHARGED?

*Sometimes, I feel exhausted.*
*How can I revitalize my spirit?*

## THE HEART OF JESUS ANSWERS:

*Come to Me, all you who labor and are heavy laden, and I will give you rest. Take My yoke upon you and learn from Me, for I am gentle and lowly in heart, and you will find rest for your souls. For My yoke is easy and My burden is light.*

MATTHEW 11:28-30 NKJV

JESUS

―――――― ⚬❦⚬ ――――――

When we genuinely lift our hearts and prayers to God, He renews our strength. Are you almost too weary to lift your head? Then bow it. Offer your concerns and your fears to your Father in Heaven. He is always at your side, offering His love and His strength.

Are you troubled or anxious? Take your anxieties to God in prayer. Are you weak or worried? Delve deeply into God's Holy Word and sense His presence in the quiet moments of the early morning. Are you spiritually exhausted? Call upon fellow believers to support you, and call upon Christ to renew your spirit and your life. Your Savior will never let you down. To the contrary, He will always lift you up if you ask Him to. So what, dear friend, are you waiting for?

God wants to give you peace, and He wants to renew your spirit. It's up to you to slow down and give Him a chance to do so.

---

**The Scripture is abundant and clear:
Christ came not only to pardon us,
but also to heal us. He wants the glory restored.**

JOHN ELDREDGE

---

## THE HEART OF JESUS PRAYS:

*Father, humans so often feel that they should have an endless supply of energy. They seem to sometimes think that to need time to rest or seek solitude shows weakness, even spiritual weakness. At times of exhaustion, may Your Spirit lead Your children into rest. Give them extra times of deep slumber and peaceful rest so they can walk in close, renewed fellowship with You and others.*

# 68

---

SADNESS

# RAINY DAYS AND MONDAYS

---

*If I'm to rejoice always, as scripture teaches,
how do I deal with sorrow?*

## THE HEART OF JESUS ANSWERS:

*So you also have sorrow now. But I will see you again. Your hearts will rejoice, and no one will rob you of your joy.*

JOHN 16:22 HCSB

JESUS

---

Grief visits all of us who live long and love deeply. When we lose a loved one, or when we experience any other profound loss, darkness overwhelms us for a while, and it seems as if we cannot summon the strength to face another day—but with God's help, we can.

When our friends or family members encounter life-shattering events, we struggle to find words that might offer them comfort and support. But finding the right words can be difficult, if not impossible. Sometimes, all that we can do is to be with our loved ones, offering them few words but much love.

Thankfully, God promises that He is "close to the brokenhearted" (Psalm 34:18 NIV). In times of intense sadness, we must turn to Him, and we must encourage our friends and family members to do likewise. When we do, our Father comforts us and, in time, He heals us.

God can dry your tears if you let Him. And, if you haven't yet allowed Him to begin His healing process, today is the perfect day to start.

---

**God is good, and heaven is forever.
These two facts should brighten up
even the darkest day.**

MARIE T. FREEMAN

---

## THE HEART OF JESUS PRAYS:

*Father, protect Your children from struggling with guilt on sad days. Help them know that rejoicing in You is an act of faith at times, instead of an emotion. Let them realize that You have created them with emotions and that it's okay to be sad at times. Let this dear child know that when he or she is grieving, You are holding on tightly and ready to comfort.*

## 69

---

SELF-WORTH

# I AM MY OWN WORST CRITIC

---

*I can be very hard on myself at times.*
*Is this okay, or should I lighten up?*

## THE HEART OF JESUS ANSWERS:

*You're blessed when you're content with just who you are—no more, no less. That's the moment you find yourselves proud owners of everything that can't be bought.*

MATTHEW 5:5 MSG

JESUS

What do you tell yourself about yourself? When you look in the mirror, are you staring back at your biggest booster or your harshest critic? If you can learn to give yourself the benefit of the doubt—if you can learn how to have constructive conversations with the person you see in the mirror—then your self-respect will tend to take care of itself. But, if you're constantly berating yourself—if you're constantly telling yourself that you can't measure up—then you'll find that self-respect is always in short supply.

Thoughts are intensely powerful things. Your thoughts have the power to lift you up or drag you down; they have the power to energize you or deplete you, to inspire you to greater accomplishments, or to make those accomplishments impossible.

The Bible teaches you to guard your thoughts against things that are hurtful or wrong (Proverbs 4:23). Yet sometimes you'll be tempted to let your thoughts run wild, especially if those thoughts are of the negative variety.

If you've acquired the habit of thinking constructively about yourself and your circumstances, congratulations. But if you're mired in the mental quicksand of overly self-critical thoughts, it's time to change your thoughts . . . and your life.

---

**If you ever put a price tag on yourself,
it would have to read "Jesus" because
that is what God paid to save you.**

JOSH MCDOWELL

---

## THE HEART OF JESUS PRAYS:

*Father, the enemy is constantly attacking Your children—telling them they're failures and that they're unacceptable to You. Give Your child the courage to hear beyond that voice of condemnation. May Your Spirit draw this child into Your Word so this one can see how deeply You love each of Your children.*

# 70

SERVICE

# I DON'T SERVE
# LIKE I SHOULD

*The world is a difficult place, and so many
people need help. How can I meet their needs?*

## THE HEART OF JESUS ANSWERS:

*The greatest among you must be a servant. But those who exalt themselves will be humbled, and those who humble themselves will be exalted.*

MATTHEW 23:11-12 NLT

JESUS

❧❦❧

J esus teaches that the most esteemed men and women are not the leaders of society or the captains of industry. To the contrary, Jesus teaches that the greatest among us are those who choose to minister and to serve.

Today, you may feel the temptation to build yourself up in the eyes of your neighbors. Resist that temptation. Instead, serve your neighbors quietly and without fanfare. Find a need and fill it . . . humbly. Lend a helping hand and share a word of kindness . . . anonymously.

Today, take the time to minister to those in need. Then, when you have done your best to serve your neighbors and to serve your God, you can rest comfortably knowing that in the eyes of God you have achieved greatness. And God's eyes, after all, are the only ones that really count.

God wants you to serve Him now, not later. Don't put off until tomorrow the good works you can perform today.

---

We worship God through service.
The authentic server views each opportunity
to lead or serve as an opportunity to worship God.

BILL HYBELS

---

## THE HEART OF JESUS PRAYS:

*Father, the enemy tells Your children not to involve them-selves with others . . . not to meet the little everyday needs of those around them. Teach Your beloved children the joy of service . . . the thrill of being Your hands and feet in meeting the needs of those around them.*

# 71

---

STRENGTH

# I NEED STRENGTH

---

*Sometimes I feel like my strength is almost gone.*
*What can I do in the moments of weakness?*

## THE HEART OF JESUS ANSWERS:

*Come to Me, all you who are weary and burdened, and I will give you rest. Take My yoke upon you and learn from Me, because I am gentle and humble in heart, and you will find rest for your souls. For My yoke is easy and My burden is light.*

MATTHEW 11:28-30 HCSB

JESUS

God is a never-ending source of strength and courage when we call upon Him. When we are weary, He gives us strength. When we see no hope, God reminds us of His promises. When we grieve, God wipes away our tears.

Do you feel burdened by today's responsibilities? Do you feel pressured by the ever-increasing demands of modern life? Then turn your concerns and your prayers over to God. He knows your needs, and He has promised to meet those needs. Whatever your circumstances, God will protect you and care for you if you allow Him to preside over your life.

Today, invite God into your heart and allow Him to renew your spirits. When you trust Him and Him alone, He will never fail you.

Life can be challenging, but fear not. God loves you, and He will protect you. Whatever your challenge, God can handle it. Let Him.

God can give you all the strength you need. Trust the Father, and trust Jesus Christ.

---

A divine strength is given to those
who yield themselves to the Father and
obey what He tells them to do.
WARREN WIERSBE

---

## THE HEART OF JESUS PRAYS:

*Father, when Your child feels weak and exhausted and helpless, may Your Spirit send the reminder that there isn't anything a human cannot do with Your help and power. Please make this eternal truth a reality in this beloved child's life.*

# 72

TALENTS

# I'M NOT REALLY USING THE TALENTS GOD GAVE ME

*God has given me special talents*
*and unique opportunities.*
*How can I know I'm being faithful with them?*

## THE HEART OF JESUS ANSWERS:

*His master said to him, "Well done, good and faithful slave! You were faithful over a few things; I will put you in charge of many things. Enter your master's joy!"*

MATTHEW 25:21 HCSB

JESUS

G od knew precisely what He was doing when He gave you a unique set of talents and opportunities. And now, God wants you to use those talents for the glory of His kingdom. So here's the $64,000 question: will you use those talents, or not?

Our Heavenly Father instructs us to be faithful stewards of the gifts that He bestows upon us. But we live in a world that encourages us to do otherwise. Ours is a society that is filled to the brim with countless opportunities to squander our time, our resources, and our talents. So we must watch for distractions and temptations that might lead us astray.

If you're sincerely interested in building a successful career, build it upon the talents that God (in His infinite wisdom) has given you. Don't try to build a career around the talents you wish He had given you.

God has blessed you with unique opportunities to serve Him, and He has given you every tool that you need to do so. Today, accept this challenge: value the talent that God has given you, nourish it, make it grow, and share it with the world. After all, the best way to say "Thank You" for God's gifts is to use them.

God has given you unique talents and opportunities. Please use them.

---

**If you want to reach your potential,
you need to add a strong work ethic to your talent.**
JOHN MAXWELL

---

## THE HEART OF JESUS PRAYS:

*Father, open Your child's eyes to see that their strengths always come from Your loving heart! May Your Spirit guide Your children to use the gifts You have given them . . . to strengthen their own faith, to live fulfilled lives, and to build Your kingdom.*

# 73

## TEMPTATION

# I CAN'T RESIST TEMPTATION

*This world is filled with temptations.*
*How can I be strong enough to overcome them?*

## THE HEART OF JESUS ANSWERS:

*Stay awake and pray, so that you won't enter into temptation. The spirit is willing, but the flesh is weak.*

MATTHEW 26:41 HCSB

JESUS

Have you noticed that this world is filled to the brim with temptations? Unless you've lived the life of a hermit, you've seen that temptations are everywhere.

Some temptations are small; eating a second scoop of ice cream, for example, is tempting, but not very dangerous. Other temptations are not nearly so harmless. The devil is working 24/7, and he's causing pain and heartache in more ways than ever before. Thankfully, in the battle against Satan, we are never alone. God is always with us, and He gives us the power to resist temptation whenever we ask Him for the strength to do so.

In a letter to believers, Peter offered a stern warning: "Your adversary the devil walks about like a roaring lion, seeking whom he may devour" (1 Peter 5:8 NKJV). As Christians, we must take that warning seriously, and we must behave accordingly.

Because you live in a temptation-filled world, you must guard your eyes, your thoughts, and your heart—all day, every day.

---

**It is easier to stay out of temptation
than to get out of it.**
RICK WARREN

---

## THE HEART OF JESUS PRAYS:

*Father, when Your children face temptation, remind them of Your words in 1 Corinthians 10:13 . . . that they can trust You to keep the temptation from becoming so strong that they think they have to give in. May Your Spirit remind them of the truth of James 4:7, that if they submit to You and resist the devil, he will flee from them. May Your children remember that through You, they are stronger than the enemy, and may they remember the enemy is the Father of lies, while You're the Father of truth and life and success.*

74

TESTIMONY

# TELL YOUR STORY

*Why is it important for me to share
my faith with others?*

## THE HEART OF JESUS ANSWERS:

*All those who stand before others and say they believe in me,*
*I will say before my Father in heaven that they belong to me.*

MATTHEW 10:32 NCV

JESUS

—⁓⁓⁓✦⁓⁓⁓—

A mong the greatest gifts we can give to our friends or family members is a willingness to share our testimonies. But sometimes, because we are afraid that we might be rebuffed, we may be slow to acknowledge the changes that Christ has made in our lives.

In his second letter to Timothy, Paul shares a message to believers of every generation when he writes, "God has not given us a spirit of timidity" (1:7). Paul's meaning is crystal clear: When sharing our testimonies, we, as Christians, must be courageous, forthright, and unashamed.

We live in a world that desperately needs the healing message of Christ Jesus. Every believer, each in his or her own way, bears responsibility for sharing the Good News of our Savior. It is important to remember that we bear testimony through both words and actions.

Billy Graham observed, "Our faith grows by expression. If we want to keep our faith, we must share it." If you are a follower of Christ, the time to express your belief in Him is now. You know how He has touched your heart; help Him do the same for others.

Because you have chosen to follow Christ, you have an important story to tell: yours.

---

**Although our actions have nothing to do with gaining our own salvation, they might be used by God to save somebody else! What we do really matters, and it can affect the eternities of people we care about.**

BILL HYBELS

---

## THE HEART OF JESUS PRAYS:

*Father, the enemy uses every trick in his arsenal to keep Your children from telling others what You have done for them. May Your Spirit help them find the courage, the strength, and the overwhelming desire to let others know how You have helped them and how You can help others.*

# 75

---

## THANKSGIVING

# SAY "THANKS"
# TO GOD

---

*I have so much to be thankful for.*
*How can I express my gratitude to God?*

## THE HEART OF JESUS ANSWERS:

*Love the Lord your God with all your passion and prayer and intelligence. This is the most important, the first on any list. But there is a second to set alongside it: Love others as well as you love yourself. These two commands are pegs; everything in God's Law and the Prophets hangs from them.*

MATTHEW 22:35-40 MSG

JESUS

As believers who have been touched by God's grace, we are blessed beyond measure. God sent His only Son to die for our sins. And God has given us the priceless gifts of eternal love and eternal life. We, in turn, are instructed to approach our Heavenly Father with reverence and thanksgiving.

Sometimes, life on earth can be complicated and exhausting. When the demands of life leave us rushing from place to place, we may fail to pause and thank our Creator for the countless blessings He bestows upon us. Whenever we neglect to give proper thanks to the Giver of all things good, we suffer because of our misplaced priorities. But when we slow down and express our gratitude to the One who made us, we enrich our own lives and the lives of those around us.

Thanksgiving should become a habit, a regular part of our daily routines. Yes, God has blessed us beyond measure, and we owe Him everything, including our eternal praise . . . starting now.

---

**Thanksgiving or complaining—these words express two contrastive attitudes of the souls of God's children in regard to His dealings with them. The soul that gives thanks can find comfort in everything; the soul that complains can find comfort in nothing.**

HANNAH WHITALL SMITH

---

## THE HEART OF JESUS PRAYS:

*Father, open the eyes of Your children to see how You are working in their lives every day. When busy times or worry or anything else tries to block their ability to see Your grace, help them slow down and see Your glorious works. May they learn to praise You for each display of You and Your power in their lives—whether small or large.*

# 76

## THOUGHTS

# MY THOUGHTS GET HIJACKED BY FEAR AND NEGATIVITY

*Sometimes, my thoughts are negative or fearful.*
*How can I change this?*

## THE HEART OF JESUS ANSWERS:

*Those who are pure in their thinking are happy, because they will be with God.*

MATTHEW 5:8 NCV

JESUS

D o you pay careful attention to the quality of your thoughts? And are you careful to direct those thoughts toward topics that are uplifting, enlightening, and pleasing to God? If so, congratulations. But if your thoughts are hijacked from time to time by the negative influences and attitudes that have invaded our troubled world, you are not alone. Ours is a society that focuses on—and often glamorizes—the negative aspects of life. That's unfortunate.

God intends that you experience joy and abundance. So, today and every day hereafter, celebrate the life that God has given you by focusing your thoughts upon those things that are worthy of praise (Philippians 4:8). And while you're at it, count your blessings instead of your hardships. When you do, you'll undoubtedly offer words of thanks to your Heavenly Father for gifts that are simply too numerous to count.

Your thoughts have the power to lift you up or bring you down, so you should guard your thoughts very carefully.

———⚜———

**The things we think are the things that feed our souls. If we think on pure and lovely things, we shall grow pure and lovely like them; and the converse is equally true.**
HANNAH WHITALL SMITH

———⚜———

## THE HEART OF JESUS PRAYS:

*Father, so many times Your children move beyond realism to negativism. Help them remember that You are the Father of all good things. Therefore they can expect and find good from You. Even when negative things happen, may Your Spirit remind them that through You, all things can be made new . . . and good!*

## 77

TRUSTING GOD

# HOW DO I TRUST
# A GOD I CAN'T SEE?

*What should I do when
I have a hard time trusting God?*

## THE HEART OF JESUS ANSWERS:

*Do not let your hearts be troubled. Trust in God; trust also in me. In my Father's house are many rooms; if it were not so, I would have told you. I am going there to prepare a place for you.*

JOHN 14:1-2 NIV

JESUS

* * *

**W**here will you place your trust today? Will you trust in the ways of the world, or will you trust in the Word and the will of your Creator?

If you aspire to do great things for God's kingdom, you will trust Him completely.

Trusting God means trusting Him in every aspect of your life. You must trust Him with your relationships. You must trust Him with your finances. You must follow His commandments and pray for His guidance. Then, you can wait patiently for God's revelations and for His blessings.

When your trust your Heavenly Father without reservation, you can rest assured: in His own fashion and in His own time, God will bless you in ways that you never could have imagined. So trust Him, and then prepare yourself for the abundance and joy that will most certainly be yours through Him.

Because God is trustworthy—and because He has made promises to you that He intends to keep—you are protected.

———❦———

**Trusting in my own mental understanding becomes a hindrance to complete trust in God.**
OSWALD CHAMBERS

———❦———

## THE HEART OF JESUS PRAYS:

*Father, help Your children to practice faith in You in the small areas of their lives . . . all through each day. Help them turn to You as an act of confidence in Your powers and abilities. Help them to call upon You when they face doubts. And help them understand that faith is not an emotion— they don't have to feel Your presence to know it's there. Help them learn that this is what trust is all about.*

# 78

WORK

# WORK TO DO

*Sometimes, it's tempting to avoid
my responsibilities.
What's the problem with taking a break?*

## THE HEART OF JESUS ANSWERS:

*The harvest truly is plentiful, but the laborers are few.*

JESUS

---

The world often promises instant gratification: Get rich—today. Lose weight—this week. Have whatever you want—right now. Yet life's experiences and God's Word teach us that the best things in life require heaping helpings of both time and work.

In life there are no shortcuts to any place worth going. So it's important to remember that hard work is not simply a proven way to get ahead, it's also part of God's plan.

When you work hard, you'll feel better about yourself and your world. When you summon the strength to keep going, even when you'd rather quit, you'll be rewarded.

So, today, do yourself this favor: Don't look for short-cuts (because there aren't any) and don't expect easy solutions to life's big challenges (because big rewards usually require lots of effort). You inhabit a world in which instant gratification is rare, but the rewards of hard work are not. Shape your expectations—and your work habits—accordingly.

The Lord has things He wants you to accomplish before He calls you home. When you find work that pleases God—and when you apply yourself conscientiously to the job at hand—you'll be rewarded.

———⟨◦⟩———

**Ordinary work, which is what most of us do most of the time, is ordained by God every bit as much as is the extraordinary.**
ELISABETH ELLIOT

———⟨◦⟩———

## THE HEART OF JESUS PRAYS:

*Father, help Your child to remember that life, including the spiritual walk, is a process. At times results and rewards come quickly, but more often they don't. May Your Spirit help Your child patiently work through the process.*

# 79

WORLDLINESS

# IN THE WORLD,
# BUT NOT
# OF THE WORLD

*This world can be a dangerous place.*
*What advice do you have?*

## THE HEART OF JESUS ANSWERS:

*Don't collect for yourselves treasures on earth, where moth and rust destroy and where thieves break in and steal. But collect for yourselves treasures in heaven, where neither moth nor rust destroys, and where thieves don't break in and steal. For where your treasure is, there your heart will be also.*

MATTHEW 6:19-21 HCSB

JESUS

e live in the world, but we should not worship it—yet at every turn, or so it seems, we are tempted to do otherwise. As Warren Wiersbe correctly observed, "Because the world is deceptive, it is dangerous."

The 21st-century world we live in is a noisy, distracting place, a place that offers countless temptations and dangers. The world seems to cry, "Worship me with your time, your money, your energy, your thoughts, and your life!" But if we are wise, we won't fall prey to that temptation.

C. S. Lewis said, "Aim at heaven and you will get earth thrown in; aim at earth and you will get neither."

That's good advice. You're likely to hit what you aim at, so aim high . . . aim at heaven.

Your world is full of distractions and temptations. Your challenge is to live in the world but not be of the world.

---

**We need more love for the Word
and less love for the world.**

R. G. LEE

---

## THE HEART OF JESUS PRAYS:

*Father, help Your dear one realize that You have put him or her in the world for a reason, for an eternal reason. As this child walks through days on earth may he or she focus on You and trust You to guide and direct each step.*

80

---

WORRY

# BEYOND WORRY

---

*When I'm overcome by worries,*
*what should I do . . . and where should I turn?*

## THE HEART OF JESUS ANSWERS:

*So don't worry, saying, "What will we eat?" or "What will we drink?" or "What will we wear?" For the Gentiles eagerly seek all these things, and your heavenly Father knows that you need them. But seek first the kingdom of God and His righteousness, and all these things will be provided for you. Therefore don't worry about tomorrow, because tomorrow will worry about itself. Each day has enough trouble of its own.*

MATTHEW 6:31-34 HCSB

JESUS

Because we are imperfect, we worry. Even though we have been given the assurance of salvation—even though we have received the promise of God's love and protection—we end up fretting over the countless details of everyday life. Jesus understood our concerns when He spoke the reassuring words found in Matthew 6: "Therefore I tell you, do not worry about your life . . ."

As you consider the promises of Jesus, remember that God still sits in His heaven and you are His beloved child. Then, perhaps, you will worry a little less and trust God a little more, and that's as it should be because God is trustworthy and you are protected. Instead of worrying about tomorrow, trust God today . . . and every day.

---

**God is bigger than your problems.**
**Whatever worries press upon you today,**
**put them in God's hands and leave them there.**
BILLY GRAHAM

---

## THE HEART OF JESUS PRAYS:

*Father, when people look at life from a human perspective there's so much to reasonably worry about. Help this dear one of Yours look at the world through Your eyes and through a filter of Your possibilities. May Your Spirit fill this one with hope and reassurance that You have everything in control, now and forever.*

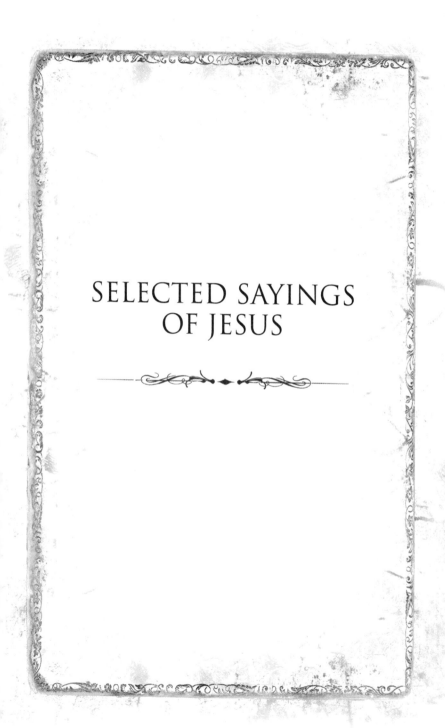

# SELECTED SAYINGS
## OF JESUS

# WHAT JESUS SAYS ABOUT . . .
## ADVERSITY

*In this world you will have trouble. But take heart! I have overcome the world.*

JOHN 16:33 NIV

*Come to me, all you who are weary and burdened, and I will give you rest. Take my yoke upon you and learn from me, for I am gentle and humble in heart, and you will find rest for your souls. For my yoke is easy and my burden is light.*

MATTHEW 11:28-30 NIV

## ASKING GOD FOR HELP

*I assure you: The one who believes in Me will also do the works that I do. And he will do even greater works than these, because I am going to the Father. Whatever you ask in My name, I will do it, so that the Father may be glorified in the Son. If you ask Me anything in My name, I will do it.*

JOHN 14:12-14 HCSB

*And in that day you will ask Me nothing. Most assuredly, I say to you, whatever you ask the Father in My name He will give you. Until now you have asked nothing in My name. Ask, and you will receive, that your joy may be full.*

JOHN 16:23-24 NKJV

## COURAGE

But Jesus beheld them, and said unto them, "With men this is impossible; but with God all things are possible."

MATTHEW 19:26 KJV

And he saith unto them, Why are ye fearful, O ye of little faith? Then he arose, and rebuked the winds and the sea; and there was a great calm. But the men marvelled, saying, What manner of man is this, that even the winds and the sea obey him!

MATTHEW 8:26-27 KJV

## FAITH

I assure you: If anyone says to this mountain, "Be lifted up and thrown into the sea," and does not doubt in his heart, but believes that what he says will happen, it will be done for him.

MARK 11:23 HCSB

Everything is possible to the one who believes.

MARK 9:23 HCSB

## WHAT JESUS SAYS ABOUT . . .
## DISCIPLESHIP

*Whoever serves me must follow me. Then my servant will be with me everywhere I am. My Father will honor anyone who serves me.*

JOHN 12:26 NCV

*Whoever is not willing to carry the cross and follow me is not worthy of me. Those who try to hold on to their lives will give up true life. Those who give up their lives for me will hold on to true life.*

MATTHEW 10:38-39 NCV

## FORGIVENESS

*Then Peter came to him and asked, "Lord, how often should I forgive someone who sins against me? Seven times?" "No!" Jesus replied, "seventy times seven!"*

MATTHEW 18:21-22 NLT

*Judge not, and ye shall not be judged: condemn not, and ye shall not be condemned: forgive, and ye shall be forgiven.*

LUKE 6:37 KJV

## GENEROSITY

*If you give, you will receive. Your gift will return to you in full measure, pressed down, shaken together to make room for more, and running over. Whatever measure you use in giving—large or small—it will be used to measure what is given back to you.*

LUKE 6:38 NLT

*Freely you have received, freely give.*

MATTHEW 10:8 NIV

## GREED

*And He told them, "Watch out and be on guard against all greed, because one's life is not in the abundance of his possessions."*

LUKE 12:15 HCSB

*No servant can be the slave of two masters, since either he will hate one and love the other, or he will be devoted to one and despise the other. You can't be slaves to both God and money.*

LUKE 16:13 HCSB

## WHAT JESUS SAYS ABOUT . . .
## HEAVEN

*Let not your heart be troubled: ye believe in God, believe also in me. In my Father's house are many mansions: if it were not so, I would have told you. I go to prepare a place for you. And if I go and prepare a place for you, I will come again, and receive you unto myself; that where I am, there ye may be also.*

JOHN 14:1-3 KJV

*Be glad and rejoice, because your reward is great in heaven.*

MATTHEW 5:12 HCSB

## LIFE

*And Jesus said unto them, I am the bread of life: he that cometh to me shall never hunger; and he that believeth on me shall never thirst.*

JOHN 6:35 KJV

*Whoever finds his life will lose it, and whoever loses his life for my sake will find it.*

MATTHEW 10:39 NIV

## PEACE

*Peace I leave with you. My peace I give to you; not as the world gives do I give to you. Let not your heart be troubled, neither let it be afraid.*

JOHN 14:27 NKJV

*I have told you these things so that in Me you may have peace. In the world you have suffering. But take courage! I have conquered the world.*

JOHN 16:33 HCSB

## RIGHTEOUSNESS

*Blessed are those who hunger and thirst for righteousness, for they will be filled.*

MATTHEW 5:6 NIV

*But seek first the kingdom of God and His righteousness, and all these things shall be added to you.*

MATTHEW 6:33 NKJV

*I am the Alpha and the Omega,*
*the Beginning and the End.*
*I will give to the thirsty from*
*the spring of living water as a gift.*

—

REVELATION 21:6 HCSB